D0582190

THROUGH THE BIBLE IN A YEAR

DENNIS LENNON

A SPIRITUAL JOURNAL

SCRIPTURE UNION

Text © Dennis Lennon 1997
Syllabus © Scripture Union 1997

First published 1997

ISBN 1 85999 196 3

British Library Cataloguing-in-
Publication Data
A catalogue record for this book is
available from the British Library.

Cover illustration by George Barr.
Design by Mark Carpenter Design
Consultants.

Printed and bound in Great Britain by
Halcyon Print & Design, Heathfield,
East Sussex.

CONTENTS

ACKNOWLEDGEMENTS

- *An Approach to Prayer*: Hubert von Zeller, Sheed & Ward (US), 1980.
- Hans Urs von Balthasar, *The Grain of Wheat: Aphorisms*, Ignatius Press (US), 1995, pp 98, 109, 113, 127. Used by permission of the publishers.
- David Bosch, *Transforming Mission*, Orbis Books (US), 1992.
- *Celebrating Common Prayer*, The Society of St Francis, © Mowbray (an imprint of Cassell plc), 1992.
- Emily Dickinson: reprinted by permission of the publishers and the Trustees of Amherst College from *The Poems of Emily Dickinson*, Thomas H Johnson (ed), Cambridge, Mass, The Belknap Press of Harvard University Press, copyright © 1951, 1955, 1979, 1983 by the President and Fellows of Harvard College; Copyright 1929, 1935 by Martha Dickinson Bianchi, copyright © renewed 1957, 1963 by Mary L Hampson, by permission of Little, Brown and Company (Inc).
- Austin Farrer: *Said or Sung*, Faith Press, 1960, p 18; *The Revelation of St John the Divine*, Oxford, 1964; *The Brink of Mystery*, SPCK, 1976, p 67.
- John Finney, taken from *Recovering the Past*, published and copyright 1996 by Darton, Longman and Todd Ltd and used by permission of the publishers.
- Daniel Hardy and David Ford: taken from *Jubilate*, published and copyright 1984 by Darton, Longman and Todd Ltd and used by permission of the publishers.
- Lawrence Kushner, *God was in this Place*, Jewish Lights Publishing (US), 1993, pp 103, 117, 123.
- Terence McCaughey: from David Brown and Ann Loades (eds), *The Sense of the Sacramental*, SPCK, 1995, p 189.
- George MacDonald: from C S Lewis (ed), *George MacDonald: An Anthology*, Geoffrey Bles: The Centenary Press, an imprint of HarperCollins Publishers, 1946, pp 67, 70, 110.
- Lesslie Newbigin, *The Open Secret*, SPCK, 1995.
- John O'Donnell SJ, *Hans Urs von Balthasar*, Geoffrey Chapman (an imprint of Cassell plc), 1992.
- John Robinson: from Robert Warren, *Building Missionary Congregations*, Church House Publishing, 1995.
- J W N Sullivan: originally published in *A New Year of Grace*, Victor Gollancz, 1961; this extract is from Richard Harries, *Art and the Beauty of God*, Mowbray, 1994, p 92. All attempts to trace the copyright holder were unsuccessful.
- Eugene Warren: from Thomas Howard, *Chance or the Dance?*, Ignatius Press (US), 1992. Used by permission of the publishers.

In the fullness of time we will have eternity for our playground. But for the present we have only our days – our precious, precarious, perishable, unrepeatable, few days. Days that are our stepping-stones into the life of God and, thereby, into our own meaning and destiny.

We have no other stepping stones, only these days. We have the privilege of receiving and using them as they come to us from the hands of God. They are ours, and we must take responsibility for them before the face of God. He has placed them conveniently for us, spacing them just about perfectly at 365 steps each year.

Teach us to number our days aright,
that we may gain a heart of wisdom. PSALM 90:12

Two moments in scripture define the spiritual potential of our days.

First, a man on a journey, pulled up in the middle of nowhere, exclaiming, 'Surely the Lord is in this place, and I was not aware of it … How awesome is this place! This is none other than the house of God [Beth-el]; this is the gate of heaven' (Gen 28:16–17).

Second, Jesus revealing the secret of finding Bethel-in-our-dullest-days: 'If anyone loves me, he will obey my teaching. My Father will love him, and we will come to him and make our home with him' (John 14:23,24).

Thus you have the potential to become 'Bethel' – God's habitation, the place where Father and Son choose to dwell in the power of the Holy Spirit. No wonder Christians have called this experience 'the sacrament of the present moment', as the Trinity comes to the loving believer under cover of life's everyday, common stuff. Can anything now be classed as 'ordinary'?

A simple discipline is required at the heart of each day for Bethel to happen for us, even in the most unpromising of circumstances and on the most flat and stale of days: the discipline of hastening to meet the Lord in his word because we love him. Mary, Jesus' mother, is our model: she 'treasured up all these things and pondered them in her heart'. Mary, who abandoned the outcome of her life to the Lord: 'I am the Lord's servant. May it be to me as you have said' (Luke 2:19;1:38).

The pattern of daily readings offered in this journal can be the means for our Bethels, our 'gate of heaven' encounters with the Lord. He is standing even now in the midst of our days, ready to receive us into his life and purpose. Instead of setting up a pile of stones, as Jacob did, to mark the significance of what transpires in these encounters, you can simply put pen to paper and make a note each day. Over a year, you will have plotted your spiritual journey, with its lessons, prayers, key ideas, tears, revelations, complaints, ecstasies and decisions.

But perhaps you have already glanced at some of the readings, and are worrying about the amount of scripture set for each day. Why attempt to read through the whole Bible, and in just one year?

Because the message is also in the overview. If you want to examine the cement between the bricks of a building, you need to stand very close to the wall. But then you cannot tell if the structure is a police station or a cathedral. To determine that, stand well back and slowly circle the entire building. Then, for the complete picture, rise slowly, in your helicopter, above and over it. After your all-round scrutiny, you can return to examining the details, which will now be even more interesting since you have seen how everything relates to and connects with everything else.

Through the Bible in a Year will serve as your helicopter ride. On the journey you will see that the overview, the overarching story, is about the Creator, the cosmos, the covenant and Christ. As Eugene Peterson puts it: 'Whether in reading scripture or conversing around the kitchen table, an isolated sentence can only be misunderstood. The more sentences we have, the deeper the sense of narrative is embedded in our minds and imaginations, and the more understanding is available. Matthew is incomprehensible without Exodus and Isaiah … Revelation is a crossword puzzle without Ezekiel and the Psalms.'[1]

Note
1. Eugene Peterson, quoted in *Daily Notes*, April–June 1988, Scripture Union, p3.

Focus

Calm your mind, spend a few moments in silence, and focus your attention on what is about to happen as you respond to the Lord's invitation to meet him through his word today.

> *'How awesome is this place! This is none other than*
> *the house of God; this is the gate of heaven.'*

Pray

Ask the Lord to speak to you as you read. Pray that the Spirit – the 'interior master' – will make clear to you what God is saying.

Read

Don't be overwhelmed by the length of any reading. You may want to set aside some sections for another time later in the day.

The readings are arranged under themes. There are brief notes on each theme, in this first part of the journal, to help you be aware of the circumstances surrounding each passage.

Reflect

Turn your thoughts over and over in your praying mind, intermingling your own longings with the transforming spirit of God's word.

When you do this, a conversation is happening: God speaks to you through scripture and, as you ponder his words and allow them to percolate through the deeper levels of your thinking, you will find yourself breathing back your praise, prayers, requests and decisions.

Mark the encounter

The surface of ancient Israel was littered with piles of stones put there by people who had met the Lord in that place. Some found their encounter with God to be their Bethel, the gate of heaven.

Note down in the space for each day's reading the most significant thing that has arisen from it, perhaps a key verse, a prayer, a confession or a decision.

Pray

A wise teacher has said, 'No doctrine deserves its place unless it is prayable, and no Christian deserves his doctrines who does not pray them.'[1] Let your reading fuel your prayer.

1. Austin Farrer, *Lord, I Believe*, Faith Press, 1958, pp 9, 10.

One obvious way to read through the Bible would be to start at Genesis and finish with Revelation. But the Bible does not work like that. Very soon in Genesis, themes occur that are as much a concern of the New Testament as they are of the Old.

Therefore, while the analogy we often hear – that 'the Bible is a library of sixty-six books' – is helpful in describing the wide variety of literary genres reflected in God's word, it can be misleading if it fails to convey the dynamic nature of scripture. The 'library' analogy implies that we move on from the elementary, introductory volumes to the more advanced. But the Bible is not like that: every part of it needs every other part.

There are indeed promises in the Old Testament which await fulfilment in the New, symbols that look for completion and shadows that await substance. However, it is equally true that the fulfilment, completion and substance of the New Testament are almost meaningless unless we learn something of their amplitude, depth and richness from the Old. For example, what is the church triumphant singing at this moment in glory? 'The song of Moses the servant of God and the song of the Lamb' (Rev 15:3). Moses and the Exodus, Israel's entire experience recorded in scripture, travel with the New Testament church of Jesus Christ.

In fact, in the context of thinking of the Bible as a whole, a better analogy is that of a train. The engine is the unstoppable force of God's covenant purposes, which as it travels has new carriages connected to it. All the parts proceed together. Nothing is obsolete; everything connects and complements everything else.

Therefore, as each theme occurs on our journey through the Old Testament, we bring to bear on it the appropriate sections of the New. To take one example, 'Forming a covenant people' appears at Genesis 12 and at once sets off bells ringing in Hebrews, Romans and Galatians. It would be a distortion to leave those New Testament passages until we have 'finished' reading the Old Testament.

God is one. His work is one. The revelation of his work recorded in the Bible is one. Enter it where you will, you find that the rest of the Bible wants to join you at that point.

THE PROLOGUE

Chapters 1–11 form a prologue not only to the book of Genesis but to the whole Bible. You need only listen to the questions that thoughtful people ask about life to appreciate the purpose of the prologue. Indeed, our very nature of being human will draw us to search for answers to those questions, for light to be shed on the mystery of life and for power to be given us to gain mastery over life.

Because this search for knowledge is fundamental to people of every culture and every generation, because this wisdom is God's gift to the human family, the language used by the writer is universal. Universal language is pictorial, and thus it belongs to everyone and is accessible to all.

> *The writing bears much the same relation to dogmatic theology that a landscape by Turner does to an ordnance map.* BENNETT[1]

The effect is something like a stained-glass window depicting an abstract design. The design's motifs are taken up and developed in the various parts of the window. Similarly, the motifs introduced in these early chapters are pursued and enlarged on from Genesis 12 onwards.

We come to the text questioning the nature of the world, wondering about the meaning and value of our existence (Gen 1–2). We want some explanation of the strange contradictions within us as members of the human race, which French philosopher Blaise Pascal described as 'Man, the glory and the scum of the universe' (Gen 3). Few today would seriously question the reality of those tenacious powers we call 'evil' (Gen 4). We look at the population explosion and doubt if we can talk sensibly any longer of 'the human family' (Gen 5,10). Contemporary novelists and film-makers are fascinated by the 'human condition', by humanity's sense of remoteness from God and the forlornness that results from this alienation (Gen 6–8). What confidence have we that the Creator has not or will not abandon his troublesome creation (Gen 9)? Can he maintain control over his wayward, destructive, technologically brilliant children (Gen 11)?

These are everyone's concerns, and they are the stuff of the revelation we call 'the Bible'.

FORMING A COVENANT PEOPLE

The Bible's perspective is cosmic, universal, embracing 'all things' in heaven and earth. From the beginning God pledged and bound himself in a covenant with 'all life on the earth' and 'all peoples on earth' (Gen 9:17; 12:3). This is the range and the horizon of his action in world history. We must place our individual life-stories within the context of his immense story, unfolded in the Bible. We will discover, to our amazement, that our small stories are raised to significance because of the surprising way God proceeds – he chooses the few to be agents of his covenants to the many. As you read, you will notice this interest in individuals: after the flood, Noah; after Babel, Abraham; out of all nations, Israel; out of Israel's tribes, Judah; out of Judah's families, Joseph and Mary; out of all the people of the world, the church. God works out his covenant commitment to all creation by constantly narrowing down his focus. Thus he always maintains a covenant community in the world.

The emphasis is on quality – stop counting and start weighing. A covenant people are not stamped in a machine: they are formed in the hands of God. But it is not an élite club of favoured, special people who are the exclusive beneficiaries of covenant blessings (as Israel then, and some Christians now, seem to imagine). The reverse is true: God's people stand before the world as if to say, 'Look, if God can do it with people like us, he can do it for anyone!' It is a covenant based entirely on his love and grace. Covenant people carry the covenant – they are its trustees, witnesses and missionaries – on behalf of the world.

Our readings take us through the characteristics of covenant life: Abraham (1800 BC who dared to believe God for the gift of life; the covenant terms in which God unilaterally promises life and reinforces that promise with an oath (Gen 15–17; Heb 6:13–20); the Exodus deliverance (Exod 12); the 'marriage' ceremony at Sinai, where Israel said 'I will' to God's covenant offer (Exod 20); the life, death and resurrection of Jesus Christ, who was both sacrifice for atonement and living mediator of the (new) covenant for the whole cosmos; and, finally, the Holy Spirit, flooding the nations with love for God and the desire to know and follow him in covenant relationship (Heb 8,10: fulfilling the prophecies of Jeremiah and Ezekiel). The apostle Paul describes God's covenant purposes as 'creation … liberated from its bondage to decay and brought into the glorious freedom of the children of God' (Rom 8:21–23).

NEW HORIZONS

Covenant people are born travellers. Abraham is always the model: 'By faith Abraham … obeyed and went, even though he did not know where he was going' (Heb 11:8). Modern pilgrims are fascinated with the drama of Israel's journey from Sinai to Canaan. Its realism rings true: the unknown can be frightening (Num 11); the best of leaders have 'off days' (Num 12); and defeatist talk can sound more plausible than God's promises (Num 13).

Nomadic travelling, for all its hardships, is simple: not so Israel's sudden exposure to Canaanite culture (1230 BC). Here again, the modern believer will feel sympathy with the people's reactions. The indigenous tribes did not all just 'roll over' and let Israel walk in unscathed. The Philistines, particularly, were a growing power in the west. The sexual-animist nature of local Baal worship seemed to work well for an agrarian life spent largely in the fields, and looked like a colourful change to Israel's rather austere, image-less monotheism. The result was several hundred years of instability, as Israel fell into a cycle of failure (sin, idolatry), servitude, repentance and deliverance through a charismatic leader (the 'judges'). The 'new horizons', therefore, are not only the geographical sort: there are also conquests of love, faith and holiness to be made.

Born out of the miracle of the cross, resurrection and Pentecost, the young church was immediately on the move (Acts 8). At her best, the church has always known that faithfulness to her Lord will involve her leaving settled security to reach out with the gospel. Christ's church is a movement, not an institution. For the first Christians, as for Israel during the Exodus, external circumstances were instrumental in driving them out of Jerusalem, from the confining, suspicious boundaries of Judeo-Christianity that threatened to hold back the gospel from the Gentiles (Acts 15).

In pagan society, the church strove for 'mission to the world without worldliness in their mission'. The Corinthian epistle shows how fierce this struggle can be and how easily fashionable attitudes – intellectual, moral and mystical – infiltrate the church. In fact, most of the problems at Corinth were created by things as commonplace as pride and lack of love (1 Cor 13). More horizons were waiting to be reached.

WHERE IS THE KING?

The period of Judges ended in social chaos. The people, desperate for strong leadership to unite the tribes, demanded a king. In spite of Samuel's bleak warning (1 Sam 8), the monarchy was inaugurated with Saul. But, more than any other, it was King David who typified the ideal combination of power and goodness (1 Sam 16 – 1 Kings 2).

Almost always in the Old Testament, 'kingdom' represents not a territory but the authority and power of a king in action. Thus the reign of God is not a spatial or a static idea: it is a dynamic concept – the reign of God in action, as opposed to corrupt earthly monarchies and in contrast to all powers in heaven and earth. Its chief quality is that God is in the process of realising the ideal 'king of righteousness'. This king would be someone 'after God's own heart' (1 Sam 13:14), who would live by God's standards and abide by his law, who would protect the poor, the widows and orphans, the defenceless and weak of every kind.

Hence the enormous significance of David's reign. He broke the hold of the Philistines, united the nation, and enlarged and strengthened the borders of Israel. He did 'what was just and right for all his people' (2 Sam 8:15). God called David 'his son' and established an 'everlasting covenant' with him (2 Sam 7:11–17; 23:1–7). Long afterwards, when times got bad, people looked back to David's reign and saw in it the foreshadowing of God's future kingdom on earth.

Thus we can read Matthew and Mark alongside the Davidic history. How significant that there are 58 New Testament references to David, including the frequent title given to Jesus – 'Son of David'. Jesus announced that the longed-for kingdom had arrived with him (see Mark 1:14–15): his signs and words, his cross and resurrection, his ascension to the throne of God and the outpouring of the Holy Spirit became the mighty act of deliverance heralded by King David (Acts 2:22–36).

The kingdom of God was established in the work of Christ two thousand years ago. Our part is to point to the kingdom, to bear witness to it and celebrate it by constantly bringing the King before the gaze of the world. From one moment to another, God will draw back the curtain and the kingdom of his Son will be revealed in all creation.

FLIRTATIONS, SEDUCTIONS AND TEARS

In this grim period of Israel's history (931–587 BC), from Solomon's reign to the fall of Jerusalem and exile to Babylonia, 'flirtations with the unthinkable become routines of the unexceptional'. Solomon slowly drowned in his wholesale syncretism (1 Kings 11:1–8), and king after king went with him, seduced into an easy, often politically expedient, compromise with paganism.

Solomon's failure triggered a split: Judah (and Jerusalem) broke away from the rest of Israel (1 Kings 11:29–40). Notice the way the book of Kings presents history from the divine viewpoint, displaying the interaction between the freedom of human beings to make decisions and the freedom of God who achieves his purposes by means of, or in spite of, human choices. Through a succession of prophets, God continually injected his word of judgement and of salvation. 'In the decisive political events the initiative stems from prophets, who change the gears of history with a word of God' (Gerhard von Rad). Elijah at Carmel is a spectacular example (1 Kings 18).

Even when the Book of the Covenant was rediscovered, and the splendid King Josiah wanted to restore it to full influence, he turned to a prophetess for guidance (2 Kings 22). Josiah could, of course, read the law for himself, but the prophetic mind was required in order to discern the significance of the discovery at that particular moment in the people's history. Even then, and as a consequence of the terrible King Manasseh's apostasy, 'Judah went into captivity' (2 Kings 21).

A covenant community must, all the time, walk the fine line between evangelising the non-believing culture in which it finds itself and being seduced by it. This is why the remarkable Ecclesiastes is included under this theme. Here a believer looks at life from within the mind of the secularist and the humanist in order to lead them from futility ('meaninglessness') towards the wisdom of knowing God. Also included here is Revelation (Rev 1–3), in which the risen Lord Jesus walks among the young churches as their Prophet-King. He has specific words to direct at the unique circumstances of each church, words to encourage and to warn, words that show his people how they can wisely 'plunder the Egyptians without setting up the golden calf'. We, in our own time and place, most urgently need to hear them.

THE PROPHETS

From Amos to Jeremiah we are in the fateful period leading up to the fall of Jerusalem (587 BC) and captivity in Babylonian exile for the leading classes of the population (2 Kings 25:1–21). The prophets were not interested in bringing timeless, general, beautifully polished messages about spiritual truths. They used whatever shock tactics they thought might be effective to bring sharply focused messages directed at specific targets and intended to change the way the nation was going. The whole period became increasingly entangled in terms of national and international politics, as Israel, Judah and other small tribal nations struggled to survive against the ambitions of the Mesopotamian empires of Assyria and Babylon in the north and Egypt in the south. The prophets saw God at work within the political tensions, and called on their leaders to trust his covenant faithfulness.

Amos (760 BC) prophesied in the highly religious, morally sick society of the northern kingdom of Israel. He was scathing about the greedy, land-owning merchant class which prospered on the backs of the peasants (Amos 5:11; 8:6).

Hosea was a contemporary of Amos in Israel (which he often called 'Ephraim'). While Amos focused on the scandal of social injustice, Hosea concentrated on the sin of God's covenant people as they assimilated Canaanite Baal practices (Hos 2:5–8; 4:10–13). In his own tragic marriage, Hosea found a parable of God's heartbreak at Israel's spiritual infidelity.

Jonah This is the story of a prophet, and a story expressing concern about the spiritual condition of the school of prophets. Here is the prophetic movement in full flow of frank self-criticism. God longs to save the lost – the crew of Jonah's ship, the citizens of Nineveh. But Jonah, God's ambassador, hates the idea. For all his religious credentials, Jonah is a sinister figure, grudging, aloof, withdrawn when people around him are in danger. This is the face of self-satisfied orthodoxy. Jonah is a startling warning to the church at all times.

Micah A contemporary of Amos, Hosea and Isaiah, Micah worked mainly in the south, in Jerusalem (Mic 4:10). He targeted social injustice and pretentious religious activities that left the worshipper unchanged (Mic 3:9–11; 6:6–8).

Isaiah (740–700 BC) Chapters 1–39 of the book of Isaiah refer to the period leading to the collapse of Jerusalem. Isaiah was a contemporary of Micah, and prophesied at a time of great prosperity and much decadent luxury for the merchant and property owning classes in Jerusalem. He envisioned a glorious city in the future, to which the nations of the world would stream in order to find God (Isa 2:1–5). Isaiah's task was to keep the king steady and trusting God as stronger nations threatened Jerusalem's security.

Nahum (640 BC) prophesied against mighty Nineveh in his short message of doom, and his forewarning was fulfilled (in 612 BC). The God of Israel controls the destinies of all the nations.

Habakkuk (600 BC) Concerned about the moral problem of God using the cruel and idolatrous Chaldeans to carry out his plans, Habakkuk finds an answer in the fact that evil carries within it its own ruin. The Chaldeans would destroy themselves by their own wickedness (Hab 2:6–20).

Zephaniah (630 BC) was involved in Josiah's reforms in Jerusalem, when the Book of the Covenant was being reinstated (2 Kings 22–23). Zephaniah's message was directed at the entrenched Baal worship in Judah and among the surrounding nations. But he was no pessimist. The beautiful chapter 3 ('I will purify the lips of the peoples', v9) promises a place in God's purposes for the whole world.

Jeremiah (626–587 BC) prophesied under no less than five kings of Judah as they came and went during one of the most fateful periods in the history of the ancient Near East. Assyria was in decline, so Babylon and Egypt dominated the region. Jeremiah's hopeless task (and he gives unique insights into the sheer personal cost of someone of his temperament and spirituality accepting such a charge) was to call for uncompromising trust in God in the midst of political chaos. Jeremiah saw a time when the covenant would be drenched in the Holy Spirit and, in this sense, become a new covenant – one that creates new hearts and minds in people (Jer 31:31–34).

'BY THE RIVERS OF BABYLON'

The fall of Jerusalem, and the deportation of her leading citizens to Babylon, created an enormous crisis of faith for the covenant people. They had thought it a theological impossibility – God's elect in captivity in the pagan heartland! The prophets of exile – Ezekiel, Daniel and Isaiah – were given fresh ways of interpreting Israel's status and the purpose of her experiences.

Ezekiel (exiled 597 BC) The book opens with an astonishing symbol of God's majestic freedom over the nations. Ezekiel sees God's glorious throne as a chariot, not fixed in any one place, tradition or people (Ezek 1). As Jerusalem had discovered, no one owns or controls the presence of God: he transcends all our systems and escapes all our nets. Yet he will save his people: 'I will take you out of the nations' (Ezek 36:16–32).

God will not only forgive and restore his people, he will also work the miracle of resurrection in them (Ezek 37). Once again his glory will return on the chariot-throne to the temple (Ezek 43). This takes on cosmic significance in a stunning vision of living water flowing out from the throne to the world (Ezek 47).

Daniel Surrounded by the trappings of Babylonian power, Daniel extols the greatness of God's indestructible kingdom. God makes and unmakes kings, raises empires and pulls them down. Daniel is the representative Israelite in the nation's trials by fire and wild beast. He is God's man in the nation's sufferings. (At this point we have also included readings on God's man confronting the mystery of personal suffering – Job, in the midst of his own exile and captivity.)

Isaiah In chapters 40–55, Isaiah brought to the exiles a series of messages of preparation – disciplines of readiness – by which they could live as God's community of faith even while they were in Babylon. They had to keep alive the dynamic memories of their origins (Isa 51:1–3); avoid assimilating the Babylonian mind; criticise their idols, their myths and their politics (Isa 46–47); sing a new song in a strange land – the song of God's universal deliverance (Isa 42:10–17); claim God's great promise of life for the barren (Isa 54:1–3). And when the day came for them to make ready to go out of exile, creation would celebrate their departure (Isa 55:12–13).

JOB – ONE MAN'S EXILE
The prophets of the exile – Ezekiel, Daniel and Isaiah – spoke for God's captive people in the mystery of their suffering. In Daniel particularly, the pressure on Israel was dramatised by the three young men in the furnace and Daniel's own encounter with lions. At this point we include Job, who represents the individual believer caught in the bewilderment of apparently innocent and undeserved suffering. Israel had her exile; Job had his, and he tells it in his extraordinary story.

Job is the godly man who finds that the teachings of the wisdom tradition of his time do not cover the facts of his experience. He has lost family, home, wealth and health. His pious friends believe there must be some guilty secret in his life, which has been the cause of all his troubles. They are committed to the old understanding of the unbreakable connection between sin and suffering on the one hand, and merit and prosperity on the other. Job complains: yes, all sin does produce disorder of some sort, but not all disorder is the consequence of sin. And God remains silent.

Job's story and his conclusion do not solve 'the problem of suffering', but they make the problem more luminous. In the end – which is Job's real beginning – God takes him on a tour through nature at its most strange, pointless, perplexing and funny. He allows nature to speak for him to a man who, in his illness and isolation, is angry with the God who, for some unknown reason, seems to have turned against him.

Some profound disclosure occurs in Job's mind as he looks out on the world – something akin to the revelations given to the prophets of exile of the high majesty of God enfolding the apparently senseless present moment. But the answers must wait. 'At the end of the Job story, the solution of the plot is not the solution to the problem. Only the revelation of Christ's redemptive suffering can interpret God's mysterious ways with us' (Hans Urs von Balthasar).[2]

RETURN AND RESTORATION

Sixty-seven years after the fall of Jerusalem, the exiles were allowed home, freed by Cyrus II, the son of the Persian king who had conquered Babylon. A pagan king as God's 'shepherd', God's 'anointed', the saviour of God's people (Isa 44:28; 45:1) – this was a revolutionary idea!

The people returned to a shattered city with a shattered temple. Reconstruction at every level was vital if the nation was to rediscover its identity as a people under God's rule.

Zechariah (520 BC) concentrated on the Jerusalem temple. In visionary, prophetic symbolism, he looked at and beyond the piles of masonry to take in the immensity of God's mission in the world.

Haggai A contemporary of Zechariah's, Haggai worked to arouse the people from their exhaustion and apathy, and spur them on to restore the temple. Both he and Zechariah seem to have had a good deal of success in motivating a dispirited population.

Joel The date of Joel's ministry is uncertain, but what he said matched the felt needs of the returned exiles. He saw in the agricultural devastation around him a symbol of the deeper disorder in the life of the covenant people and of the surrounding nations. He promised fruitfulness in every way when Israel's heart returned to God, and described a final vision of future blessings.

Malachi (460 BC) Malachi's ministry took place somewhere between the volatile times of Zechariah and Haggai and the progress that Ezra and Nehemiah would later bring about. However, in Malachi's day, temple life was at very low ebb. He was able to lay the groundwork for future reforms by attacking the widespread neglect of temple worship, which had led to a lack of reverence and love for God. In one famous verse (Mal 1:11), he contrasts the pathetic worship of the covenant people with the simple sincerity of much heathen worship, a sincerity that was more acceptable to God.

The temple was eventually restored and dedicated in 516 BC. At this point in the scriptural record there is a gap of sixty years.

Ezra (458 BC) and Nehemiah (445 BC) Sixty years on, we find the temple back in the hands of a priestly elite. Ezra came from Persia to reform temple worship. He was soon followed by Nehemiah, also from Persia, whose mission was to make life and worship more secure in Jerusalem by repairing the walls against Samaritan attacks. He managed to motivate the entire population to build the wall and to protect it. They finished the task in 52 days.

Songs, prayers, wisdom and love

The psalms respond to every mood in the life of faith. There are psalms of well-being which celebrate the 'champagne moments' – 'It's good to be alive, and I thank God for it!' But there are also psalms that speak of life's 'pig-sty' moments, describing moods of confusion and despair. These have been called 'psalms of disorientation'.

In fact, much of life seems to be spent in oscillation between the two extremes as we find ourselves leaving one condition and entering the other. Therefore we are presented with many psalms of transition, in which there is a sense of lament when the movement is from light to darkness, and of joyful transformation when the pendulum swings the other way, from darkness to light. The psalms both acknowledge these swings and impact on them: we call on God to do something about our condition, or we praise him for having done so. Thus we experience doxology and lament, despair and delight, in the space of a single psalm, just like our moods. The psalms are the life of faith without pretence.

Proverbs Ancient Israel went through the process of testing and formulating what she was learning during her development as a covenant community. To manage her experiences and to communicate her findings, her teachers observed, reflected, looked for origins and causes, made connections and identified consequences. The fruit of that process they cast into 'proverbs' – brief expressions of wisdom that were easy to remember, deceptively deep, intriguing, teasing and often playful. Indeed, this is often the best package in which to deliver wisdom.

Proverbs are interpreted experiences that have been tested and confirmed, time after time, by successive generations within a stable, believing community. We do well to root our life and thought in such aids to living, so that they become signposts to guide us towards making wise decisions.

The Song of Songs Lovers will want to take this Song at face value, simply as a description of how it is between two people in love, glad that scripture should so celebrate human love. Alternatively, you may read the song as an allegory, or an extended metaphor, of God's love affair with his people. You could take it as a 'type' – the description of a real relationship between two real people, but placed in the Old Testament as a pointer to Christ's love for his church. Or you could interpret it as all three. You decide. Only consider this remarkable fact: not one major theological word of Old Testament vocabulary appears in the Song.

LIFE IN THE KINGDOM OF GOD

We have seen how the Bible is the story of the Father in search of his children. Everything in that story flows towards a single point and then radiates out from it. The death of Jesus Christ, the Son of God, on the cross circa AD 33, is that point. The cross is the power by which the King reigns; it is transforming power – like radiation from an immense explosion, streaming out from what happened when – as the church fathers put it – 'one of the Trinity died in the flesh'. In the New Testament we shall meet many different images that describe the unfathomable mystery of this event. A once-for-all-time, unique, sin-bearing, guilt-lifting, atoning death in our place, by which the Father reconciles the world to himself. Because the Son died, the Father can bring his alienated, lost children home.

In fact we will see in our readings that the work by which Christ saves is one action – from his birth, life, death, resurrection, ascension, to the outpouring of the Holy Spirit at Pentecost. The one action is like a great hammer being raised up to the highest point, before coming down to smash the prison locks and set the prisoners free. This is the power behind kingdom life – life under the King of love. Therefore, 'Jesus went into Galilee, proclaiming the good news of God. "The time has come. The kingdom of God is near. Repent and believe the good news!"' (Mark 1:14–15). From that moment, everything in Christ's ministry unfolded out of his original manifesto.

From the earliest times in the Old Testament, and in the Israel of Jesus' time, the reign of God was pictured as his protection for the help-less, the poor, the blind, the leper, the widow and the orphan (Isa 29:18; 35:3–7; 61:1–3). Thus the Gospels were making a stupendous claim when they applied Old Testament prophecy directly to Jesus as the one who fulfilled them literally and physically (Matt 10:5–8; 11:4–6; Luke 7:21–22). The Gospels saw physical disorders as symbolic of deeper spiritual disorders: when Jesus healed the paralytic man, the man's physical condition is linked to a hidden spiritual problem (Mark 2:1–12). The gospel of the kingdom is a full, holistic gospel that saves us in our spiritual-physical nature. After his resurrection, Jesus appeared to his disciples not as a ghost, but as 'I myself! Touch me and see; a ghost does not have flesh and bones, as you see I have' (Luke 24:39). The reign of God in action claims and blesses every moment of our total existence as human beings. The Epistles work out what, in practice, such a claim might mean for each one of us.

It is clear from what has been said that in every part of society there should be a living, loving demonstration of the kingdom, a context in which the things we say about the Lord are embodied and lived out. Jesus said, 'As the Father has sent me, I am sending you' (John 20:21), in flesh and blood, with spiritual realities transposed into daily life. The gospel of the kingdom needs a body. This is the function of the local church and of each Christian wherever he or she lives and works. This practical necessity is the concern of the Epistles.

Did the kingdom really and fully come with the appearance of Jesus Christ two thousand years ago? If it did, why are we to pray, 'Your kingdom come' (Matt 6:10)? If, on the other hand, the reign of God established only a foothold through Christ's life and work, then we are left with a vast and growing amount of work to do to bring in the kingdom, a crushing sense of the great 'undone'.

But this is not the atmosphere of the New Testament. We do not meet there Christians who are neurotically oppressed by evangelistic responsibilities. Rather, we are struck by the mood of joy and optimism. The solution lies in the truth that Christ is both the king and the kingdom. In fact the word 'kingdom' is a verb, the king in action. 'The kingdom has both come and is still to come because Jesus has come and is to come again' (Cranfield). Christ's victory was total and complete in his incarnation, death and resurrection, but this victory is concealed from the world – a 'veiled manifestation'. He revealed the kingdom, but not in an incontrovertible way that would leave people with no choice but to assent to it, like it or not.

The old problems persist. How can we declare to the world that our God reigns when the 'principalities and powers' seem everywhere to be in control? If we believe that Jesus is Lord over the church but not the world (that is, that the kingdom is the church), then Christ on the throne is merely a figurehead: he does not actually rule at all.

But scripture exults that he does rule over *all things* – this is fact, not fantasy. Christ is truly Lord, over everything in all creation, outside the church as well as inside.

It may be more helpful to understand the reign of God not as something slowly moving from little to much, from partial to complete, but rather from hidden to revealed, from veiled to manifest. We pray for that which is already complete to be manifest in all its glory before the eyes of all creation. Our hope, when we pray 'Your kingdom come', does not imagine a move from less to more, but from faith to sight. From one moment to the next, God snatches away the curtain and we see his reign, his kingdom, which was there all the time. So Peter speaks of 'the salvation that is ready to be revealed' (1 Pet 1:5). And, even more striking is Jesus' reference to 'the kingdom prepared for you since the creation of the world' (Matt 25:34). The Epistles help us to work out what it means to bear witness to the presence of the King (Acts 1:8) in the common stuff of our everyday lives.

WE HAVE A DESTINY

Some 354 readings ago, we entered the biblical story 'in the beginning…', at creation. The outcome is this mysterious, magnificent, tragic world. Rising above the broad expanse of scripture, our view of the overarching story becomes clearer. God the Father freely created in order to glorify his dear Son. He asked his Son to be the guarantor of creation's success in the face of a rebellious human family. The Son desires to lay everything at the Father's feet. Now the Son and the Holy Spirit work to bring all things home to the Father.

All things therefore are charged with love, are charged with God and, if we know how to touch them, give off sparks and take fire, yield drops and flow, ring and tell of Him. GERARD MANLEY HOPKINS[3]

The biblical story of redemption unfolds from the viewpoint of its climax. From the beginning, everything was attuned to the promise of God's covenant of life and guaranteed to us by Christ, its mediator. The promise goes singing through all God's unfathomable ways with his world. We sense 'the roll, the rise, the carol, the creation'.[4] We feel ourselves caught in the gravitational pull of 'the glorious freedom of the children of God ... the redemption of our bodies' (Rom 8:21–23). The cosmos will share in that moment of transfiguration of all things. Christ in his bodily resurrection assures us that we are speaking reality not fantasy when we say this.

From chapter 56 on, Isaiah speaks of the exiles returning home and the reconstruction of Jerusalem. As we read, the vision melts, glows and expands until 'Jerusalem' is no longer a pile of masonry in 500 BC, but 'a new heaven and a new earth' into which 'all mankind will come' (Isa 66:20–24). At its climax, Revelation takes Isaiah's vision and expands it to include all creation 'ransomed, healed, restored, forgiven' (Rev 21:9–27). We read Daniel 12, Matthew 24, Mark 13, 1 Corinthians 15 and Revelation in the light of the moment of transfiguration. Each chapter in its own way describes the crises, the conflicts and the quickening tempo of world history through which Christ is fulfilling his desire to bring all creation home to the Father.

Notes

1. From George A F Knight, *Theology in Pictures*, The Handsel Press Limited, 1981.
2. Hans Urs von Balthasar, *The Grain of Wheat*: Aphorisms, Ignatius Press (US), 1995.
3. Gerard Manley Hopkins, *The Poems*, Oxford University Press, 4th edition, p 263.
4. Hopkins, Poem No. 76, *The Poems*.

THE
JOURNAL

The overarching story is about Creator, cosmos, covenant, Christ.

JANUARY 1
❖ Genesis 1
❖ Psalms 1, 2

The contrast between all that is good in Genesis 1 and the wicked and rebellious in Psalms 1, 2. Yet there is one God and He is good.

JANUARY 2
❖ Genesis 2
❖ Psalms 3, 4

Man was created for God. He finds true peace only in Him. How good of God to allow us that joy and peace in Himself.

JANUARY 3
❖ Genesis 3, 4
❖ Psalm 5

The beginning of sin! Yet here we see God's plan of salvation beginning – God is never lost completely – people began to call on His Name. Also in the Psalm we see the contrast – good and evil. The good call on the Lord to praise Him & to ask for help.

JANUARY 4
❖ Genesis 5, 6
❖ Psalm 6

Obedience is what God asks for from Noah and that is what He gets. It is interesting to see how carefully instructions were given and how carefully they were carried out. God is near and very real to Noah.

God is the father in search of his children.

JANUARY **5** ❖ Genesis 7, 8
❖ Psalm 7

As Noah obeys, everything falls into place. How true for us but how hard I find that. Like David I rage futilely against things but the Lord asks for obedience and faithfulness.

JANUARY **6** ❖ Genesis 9
❖ Psalm 8

What is man, that You are mindful of him? God made a covenant and keeps it. Man is truly blessed. Today we heard of true worship — worship in the Spirit. May God grant that blessing too.

Is it chance
or dance moves the world?
Is the world blind and dumb
or bloom, festal?
A vain jest, or holy feast?

Eugene Warren

JANUARY **7** ❖ Genesis 10, 11
❖ Psalm 9

Genealogies! Yet through it all God is working. Never the obvious — not always the first son — not always the clever one. God has His own plan and He sees it through.

FORMING A COVENANT PEOPLE

JANUARY 8
❖ Genesis 12, 13
❖ Hebrews 11:1–12

Faith and faithfulness – they do go together. Abraham was human, like us he made mistakes but the main leading of his life was his faith in God.

JANUARY 9
❖ Genesis 14
❖ Hebrews 7

All history finds fulfilment in our Lord, Jesus Christ. He is our High Priest, continually praying for us and His sacrifice is sufficient.

JANUARY 10
❖ Genesis 15
❖ Galatians 1–3

The promise to Abraham, fulfilled in Christ Jesus and we are heirs of that promise. What an inheritance!!

JANUARY 11
❖ Genesis 16, 17
❖ Romans 4

Abraham and Sarah wavered but God still had His own plan and purpose. This was carried out in Isaac but Abraham still had faith in God even though he did not understand.

God will bring all creation to share in his glory.

JANUARY *12*   ❖ Genesis 18, 19
                                                ❖ Galatians 4, 5

We see Abraham's faith grow. He has the courage to plead for others and ask God to intervene. The promise is repeated and this time Sarah is unconvinced. She laughs at the idea of the desire laughing.

'God chooses and calls a community to be the messengers of his truth and bearers of his love for all people … neither truth nor love can be communicated except as they are embodied in a community which reasons and loves.'

Lesslie Newbigin

JANUARY *13*   ❖ Genesis 20, 21
                                                ❖ Galatians 6

Abraham falls into the same sin again. How like us all! God forgives him and grants the promised son. God forgives us too but we have the promise of more - life in His Son now and forever.

JANUARY *14*   ❖ Genesis 22, 23
                                                ❖ Hebrews 11:13–39

The challenge of faith — what thoughts were in Abraham's mind as he obeyed God — and that of Isaac?? Faith is not an easy option. It demands a full sacrifice and so many are mentioned in Hebrews.

FORMING A COVENANT PEOPLE

The covenant promise advances through the lives of ordinary people.

JANUARY *15*

❖ Genesis 24, 25
❖ Psalm 10

Abraham's servant shows great faith in God and a simple trust that He will lead him. Faith & trust are still asked of those who would serve Him.

JANUARY *16*

❖ Genesis 26, 27
❖ Psalm 11

Isaac receives God's promise. He shows great patience and allows himself to be moved until there is room for all. His sons are quite different from him and from each other.

JANUARY *17*

❖ Genesis 28, 29
❖ Psalm 12

How human we all are! Jacob here displays that. Esau shows it, Laban is as deceitful as Jacob and Leah is desperately human!!

JANUARY *18*

❖ Genesis 30, 31
❖ Psalm 13

God chooses to use people and we must not judge them. Jacob cheated and lied. Laban cheated Jacob several times. It was all in God's purpose and He made it to serve Him.

'What is in us is greater than we are; thus the content is greater than the vessel. Whether the vessel cracks in the enterprise or merely overflows is a matter of indifference. Only one thing matters: the tidings we bear must go forward.'

Hans Urs von Balthasar

JANUARY **19**
❖ Genesis 32, 33
❖ Psalm 14

Cautious Jacob - but God was before him and all was well. We now see him back in the Promised land ready for the next step in God's plan.

JANUARY **20**
❖ Genesis 34, 35
❖ Psalm 15

The Bible does not hide man's nature. Evil is added to evil and yet God shows His love for His people drawing them out of their sinful ways and leading them on to fulfil His purposes.

JANUARY **21**
❖ Genesis 36, 37
❖ Psalm 16

Two brothers - two family stories. One is told in a chapter. The other will take many chapters. God chooses as He will and who can stand against Him?

Joseph in Egypt: God's providence runs ahead of his people.

JANUARY *22*

❖ Genesis 38, 39
❖ Psalm 17

Joseph shows us what true faith and obedience can do. Wherever he was, in whatever adverse circumstances, he did his best and the Lord was with him.

JANUARY *23*

❖ Genesis 40, 41
❖ Psalm 18

God's timing is perfect. Joseph's confidence is amazing. He simply said that God would interpret the dream and He did. Would I have had such courage?

JANUARY *24*

❖ Genesis 42, 43
❖ Psalm 19

God's will is done in spite of man's imperfections. I wonder what Simeon thought of it all and how he was treated when he was left in Egypt.

'God does not push his creatures into existence like ducklings into a pond to sink or swim. He has a plan for them. His plans for us are what perfect wisdom suggests to infinite love; his plans for us are his love, they are all the good that his love can see for us.'

Austin Farrer

JANUARY 25

❖ Genesis 44, 45
❖ Psalm 20

Joseph tests his brothers and they are not found wanting this time. He tells them they have been part of God's plan and it was all meant to happen. He is sure of God's loving power in his life.

JANUARY 26

❖ Genesis 46, 47
❖ Psalm 21

Jacob turns to God before going down to Egypt and is encouraged to go. God's purposes are still being worked out.

JANUARY 27

❖ Genesis 48, 49
❖ Psalm 22

Jacob blesses his sons before he dies. For some the "blessing" seems not too flattering. How difficult it is to react well to unkind remarks even if they're true!!

JANUARY 28

❖ Genesis 50
❖ Psalms 23, 24

The Lord is the King of Glory. Jacob's life ended with a promise being fulfilled. Joseph's life ended with a promise given to be fulfilled later. God keeps His promise. Do I keep mine?

God saves the lost, the last and the least. He is that sort of God.

JANUARY 29

❖ Exodus 1, 2
❖ Psalm 25

"Before they call, I will answer..".
God had already prepared Moses by
saving him and giving him an education
beyond anything he could get as a slave.
God is always ready and prepared.

JANUARY 30

❖ Exodus 3, 4
❖ Psalm 26

Excuses, excuses! Moses is so
human — just like us. God became
angry with him. How much patience God
has shown with me and still does!

---

*'In a crisis our prayers are more like a groan, a gasp, a cry, an
explosion. "O God!" I cried and that was all. But what are the
prayers of the whole universe more than expansions of that one
cry? It is not what God can give us, but God that we want!'*

George MacDonald

JANUARY 31

❖ Exodus 5, 6
❖ Psalm 27

The Psalmist says "Wait for the Lord".
The Israelites & Moses were unwilling to wait
for the Lord. How willing am I? I always
want instant reaction but I must learn to wait.

FEBRUARY 1
❖ Exodus 7, 8
❖ Psalm 28

How often must God speak to us as He spoke to Pharaoh? We hear but we do not listen. We pay lip-service but when conditions improve we go our own way. But God wins through in the end.

FEBRUARY 2
❖ Exodus 9, 10
❖ Psalm 29

This could be the Middle East today or Europe — Balkan States. Give in — break promise — make promise — break promise. These are public but what are we like in private?

FEBRUARY 3
❖ Exodus 11, 12
❖ Psalm 30

At last — they are free. The Passover is established and its importance is emphasised by repeated repetition. For us — the Cross — but do we honour it in the same joyous way?

FEBRUARY 4
❖ Exodus 13, 14
❖ Psalm 31

The Lord led them — even through the Red Sea. He still leads and protects us if we but trusted Him enough we would never fear.

Like a good marriage, God's covenant with us will only work when fuelled by mutual love.

FEBRUARY **5**
❖ Exodus 15, 16
❖ Hebrews 2

Faulty memories – we all suffer from
them. We too long to return to former ways
when the going gets tough – we forget how
tough it was before ∴ God is always first's
answer.

*There is an old Jewish legend which says that the two tablets
containing the commandments, one concerning our duty to God
and the other our duty to our neighbour, came from one block of
stone; and that if fitted together, they made a perfect cube.*

FEBRUARY **6**
❖ Exodus 17, 18
❖ Hebrews 3

Moses was a great leader but he was
also humble enough to take advice from
Jethro. Hebrews reminds us that while Moses
was great, Jesus is greater and He is our
leader.

FEBRUARY **7**
❖ Exodus 19, 20
❖ Matthew 3

How privileged we are that God has
spoken to us through Jesus. We can
approach because of Him and we can
converse with the Lord.

Jesus fulfils Moses: his sermon on the mount fulfils (that is, fills to the full) the law given at Sinai.

FEBRUARY 8

❖ Exodus 21, 22
❖ Matthew 4

How sensible and wise are God's laws. His plan is for a community to live in peace and safety with due penalties for those who offend. The way of the Lord is just and good.

FEBRUARY 9

❖ Exodus 23, 24
❖ Matthew 5

The Jews found the OT laws hard. Jesus did not detract from them. Instead He seems to make them harder. The aim is to be perfect — only in Him when we see Him face to face!!

FEBRUARY 10

❖ Exodus 25, 26
❖ Matthew 6

"Each day has enough trouble of its own". That is a truth I should learn. Why do I worry? I know in theory what to do but in practice??

FEBRUARY 11

❖ Exodus 27, 28
❖ Matthew 7

Authority — God had all the plans and the measurements and gave all the instructions for the Tent and for Aaron's garments. Jesus, too, spoke with authority and all were astonished.

FORMING A COVENANT PEOPLE

Why did the Exodus take place? So that God's people would be free to offer him praise and service.

FEBRUARY *12*
❖ Exodus 29, 30
❖ Hebrews 4:14–16, 5

The anointing, robing, purifying of the High Priest is so elaborate. Approach to God is hard because all ~~to offer~~ the offerings must be made. Christ is our High Priest & His offering is perfect & complete.

FEBRUARY *13*
❖ Exodus 31, 32
❖ Hebrews 6

1) God gives gifts to His people as they are needed in His service.

2) God knows our weakness. We can so easily turn away from Him and serve other Gods. Pray for His keeping power.

'The gesture of worship is generous and beautiful … henceforth anything that takes away the gesture of worship stunts and even maims us forever. Henceforth being merely secular is servitude and inhibition. If we cannot pray we are gagged; if we cannot kneel we are in irons.'

G K Chesterton

FEBRUARY *14*
❖ Exodus 33, 34
❖ Hebrews 8

Two covenants. How blessed are we who have the new covenant and have the Lord Jesus as our friend.

Moses and Aaron established external forms of law and ceremony. Christ mediates their inner reality to us through the Holy Spirit.

FEBRUARY *15*

❖ Exodus 35, 36
❖ Hebrews 9

The people had to be restrained from giving because there was more than enough for the task. Can we imagine that in our church?

FEBRUARY *16*

❖ Exodus 37, 38
❖ Hebrews 10

What a wonderful creation the Tabernacle was BUT we have no need of it or of the endless sacrifices. Christ Jesus is sufficient as He has done it all.

FEBRUARY *17*

❖ Exodus 39
❖ 2 Corinthians 3, 4

The glory of the old is far surpassed by the glory of Christ Jesus. As we are in Him we should share to His glory. Help me to do so!

FEBRUARY *18*

❖ Exodus 40
❖ 2 Corinthians 5
❖ Psalm 32, 33

God said, "I will instruct you and teach you in the way you should go." Moses did everything as the Lord had commanded. Paul reminds us of what Christ has done. The Psalmist rejoices in the Lord's way.

Symbol: Leviticus dramatises the principle of 'the one for the many'.

FEBRUARY 19
❖ Leviticus 1–3
❖ John 1

The elaborate sacrifices are laid
out in great detail. John introduces
Jesus quietly as "The Lamb of God".

FEBRUARY 20
❖ Leviticus 4, 5
❖ John 2

The carefully laid-out sacrifices & rules
became a burden and were exploited for
profit. Jesus literally "over-turned" them
and did so figuratively as well.

FEBRUARY 21
❖ Leviticus 6, 7
❖ John 3

Belief in the Lord Jesus Christ leads
to eternal life. The careful lay-out
of the various sacrifices fore-shadow
the Cross but have no more meaning now
for us.

FEBRUARY 22
❖ Leviticus 8, 9
❖ John 4

Worship, with or without ritual,
must be sincere and must be in Spirit
and in truth.

Completion: Priest, sacrifice and mediator – Jesus is all three in himself.

FEBRUARY 23

❖ Leviticus 10, 11
❖ John 5

There is no mistake in the supreme
sacrifice of Jesus. He made it once
for all and the promise is secure.

FEBRUARY 24

❖ Leviticus 12, 13
❖ John 6

God cares for us in so many ways.
The laws for health were good and sound
and must have saved many lives.

FEBRUARY 25

❖ Leviticus 14, 15
❖ John 7

Jesus teaches His disciples with words
that come from God. They are astonished
at His teaching which they can
understand and yet cannot fully grasp.

'Leviticus seems so, well, "physical". But the Old Testament is
clear that we are a totality of body, mind and spirit. That which
is unloved tends to turn nasty, and if our bodies are neglected
and unloved they, too, will turn nasty. Much better to use our
bodies as part of our prayer.'

From *An Approach to Prayer*

Shadow: Leviticus dramatises God's concern for the wholeness of personal and community life.

FEBRUARY *26* ❖ Leviticus 16, 17
❖ John 8

FEBRUARY *27* ❖ Leviticus 18, 19
❖ John 9

FEBRUARY *28* ❖ Leviticus 20, 21
❖ John 10

MARCH *1* ❖ Leviticus 22, 23
❖ John 11

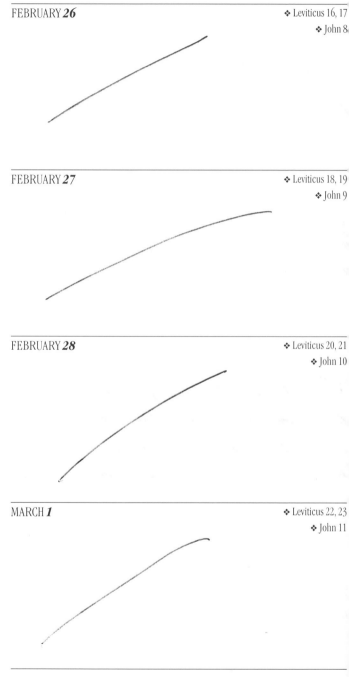

Substance: Jesus raises up damaged and lost people into new life with the Father.

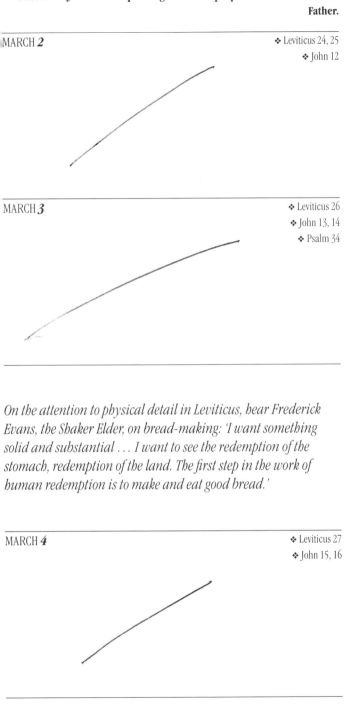

MARCH **2**

- ❖ Leviticus 24, 25
- ❖ John 12

MARCH **3**

- ❖ Leviticus 26
- ❖ John 13, 14
- ❖ Psalm 34

On the attention to physical detail in Leviticus, hear Frederick Evans, the Shaker Elder, on bread-making: 'I want something solid and substantial … I want to see the redemption of the stomach, redemption of the land. The first step in the work of human redemption is to make and eat good bread.'

MARCH **4**

- ❖ Leviticus 27
- ❖ John 15, 16

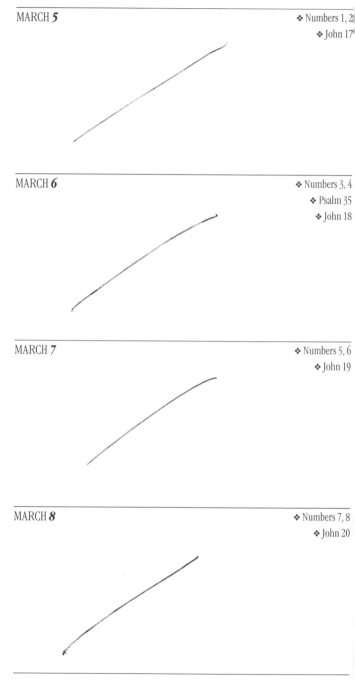

MARCH **5**
❖ Numbers 1, 2
❖ John 17

MARCH **6**
❖ Numbers 3, 4
❖ Psalm 35
❖ John 18

MARCH **7**
❖ Numbers 5, 6
❖ John 19

MARCH **8**
❖ Numbers 7, 8
❖ John 20

'Don't make yourselves too comfortable. We're leaving in the morning.'

MARCH **9**

❖ Numbers 9
❖ John 21

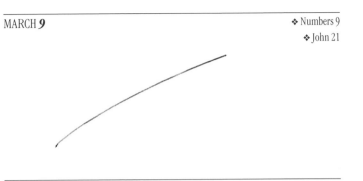

---

*'Doubts are the messengers of the Living One to the honest …
doubt must precede every deeper assurance; for uncertainties are
what we first see when we look into a region hitherto unknown,
unexplored, unannexed.'*

George MacDonald

MARCH **10**

❖ Numbers 10
❖ Acts 1, 2

MARCH **11**

❖ Numbers 11, 12
❖ Acts 3

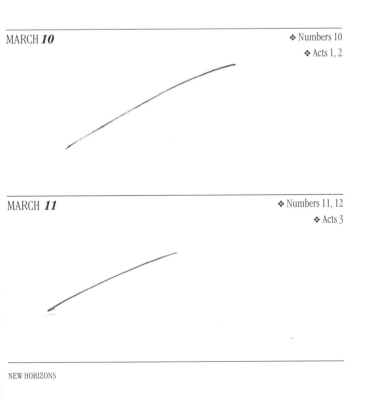

Rebellion was a catastrophe, a forty-year detour.

MARCH *12*	❖ Numbers 13, 14
	❖ Acts 4

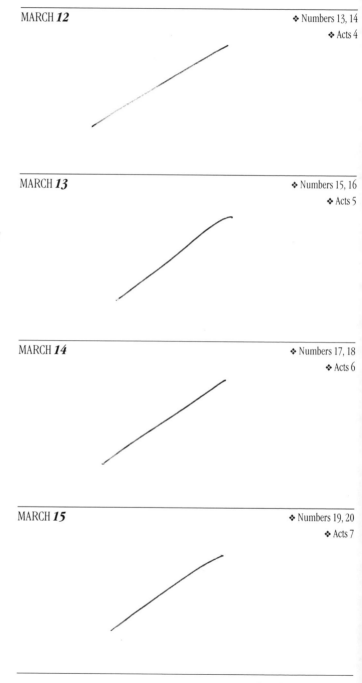

MARCH *13* ❖ Numbers 15, 16 ❖ Acts 5

MARCH *14* ❖ Numbers 17, 18 ❖ Acts 6

MARCH *15* ❖ Numbers 19, 20 ❖ Acts 7

With word, action and sign, the young church burst out of Jerusalem.

The love that characterises new life in Christ moves out in all directions, like a river bursting its banks.

'Mission has its origin in the heart of God. God is a fountain of sending love … there is mission because God loves people.'

David Bosch

MARCH **16**

❖ Numbers 21, 22
❖ Acts 8

MARCH **17**

❖ Numbers 23, 24
❖ Psalm 36
❖ Acts 9

MARCH **18**

❖ Numbers 25, 26
❖ Acts 10

Moses reviews the forty-year trek and prepares Israel for Canaan.

MARCH *19*

❖ Numbers 27, 28
❖ Acts 11

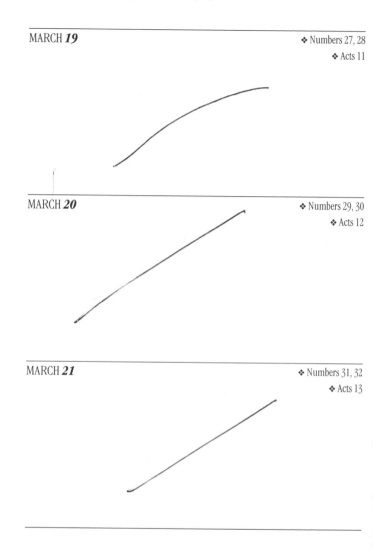

MARCH *20*

❖ Numbers 29, 30
❖ Acts 12

MARCH *21*

❖ Numbers 31, 32
❖ Acts 13

'The person who reaches out for what lies ahead of him is always becoming younger than himself ... God's commandments are to be fulfilled with an inexhaustible yearning that is ever making haste.'

Bishop Basil, fourth century

Jesus walks ahead of his people. His church is a movement, not an institution.

MARCH *22*

❖ Numbers 33, 34
❖ Acts 14

MARCH *23*

❖ Numbers 35, 36
❖ Acts 15

MARCH *24*

❖ Deuteronomy 1
❖ Psalm 37
❖ Acts 16

MARCH *25*

❖ Deuteronomy 2, 3
❖ Acts 17

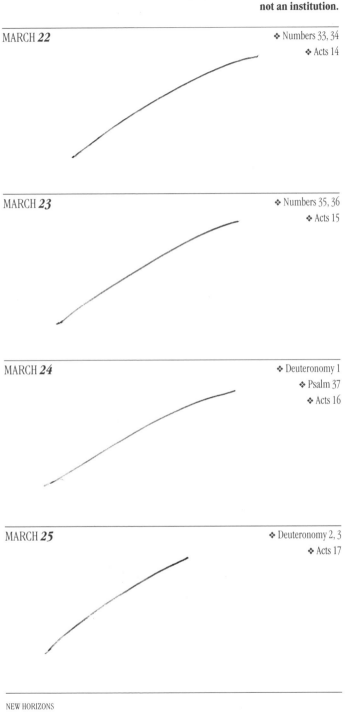

What is the law? A means of loving God totally. This love will spill over to the people around us.

MARCH *26*

❖ Deuteronomy 4, 5
❖ Acts 18

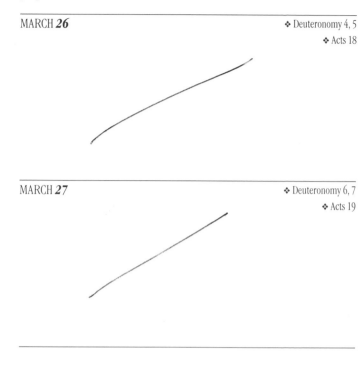

MARCH *27*

❖ Deuteronomy 6, 7
❖ Acts 19

'It is the heart that is not yet sure of its God which is afraid to laugh in his presence.'

George MacDonald

MARCH *28*

❖ Deuteronomy 8, 9
❖ Acts 20

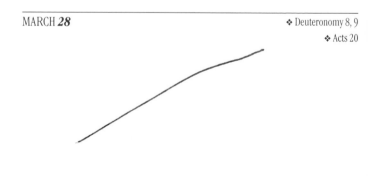

Touched by Christ's love, people become courageous and inventive in their love for the world.

MARCH **29**   ❖ Deuteronomy 10, 11
                                                 ❖ Acts 21

MARCH **30**   ❖ Deuteronomy 12, 13
                                                 ❖ Acts 22

MARCH **31**   ❖ Deuteronomy 14, 15
                                                 ❖ Psalm 38
                                                 ❖ Acts 23

APRIL **1**   ❖ Deuteronomy 16, 17
                                                 ❖ Acts 24

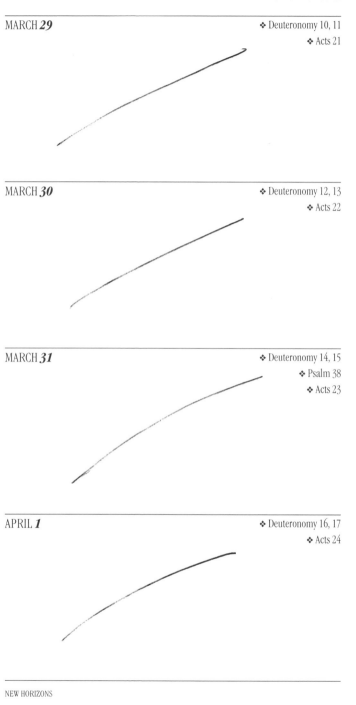

You are now the people of God – so behave as though you are!

APRIL *2*　　　　　　　　　　　　　　　　　　　❖ Deuteronomy 18, 19
　　　　　　　　　　　　　　　　　　　　　　　　❖ Acts 25

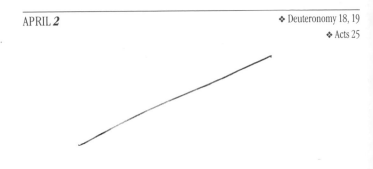

'This life is not health, but healing; not being, but becoming; not rest, but exercise. We are not yet what we shall be, but we are growing toward it; the process is not yet finished, but it is going on; this is not the end, but it is the road. All does not yet gleam in glory, but all is being purified.'

Martin Luther

APRIL *3*　　　　　　　　　　　　　　　　　　　❖ Deuteronomy 20, 21
　　　　　　　　　　　　　　　　　　　　　　　　❖ Acts 26

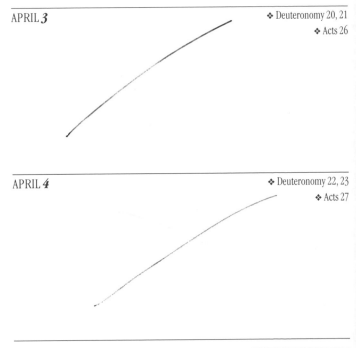

APRIL *4*　　　　　　　　　　　　　　　　　　　❖ Deuteronomy 22, 23
　　　　　　　　　　　　　　　　　　　　　　　　❖ Acts 27

The identity of a covenant community is formed in the tension between what it believes and where it lives, its theology and its culture.

APRIL 5

❖ Deuteronomy 24, 25
❖ Acts 28
❖ Psalm 39

APRIL 6

❖ Deuteronomy 26, 27
❖ Psalm 40

APRIL 7

❖ Deuteronomy 28, 29
❖ Psalm 41

APRIL 8

❖ Deuteronomy 30, 31
❖ Psalm 42

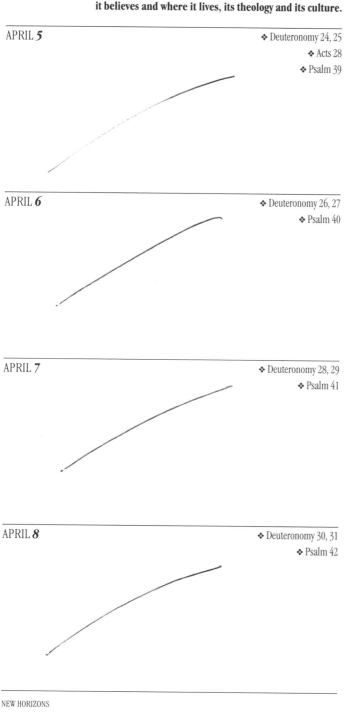

Moses and Joshua urge Israel towards 'a long obedience in the same direction'.

APRIL *9* ❖ Deuteronomy 32
❖ Psalms 43, 44

APRIL *10* ❖ Deuteronomy 33, 34
❖ Psalm 45

APRIL *11* ❖ Joshua 1, 2
❖ Hebrews 4 :1–13

APRIL *12* ❖ Joshua 3, 4
❖ Ephesians 1

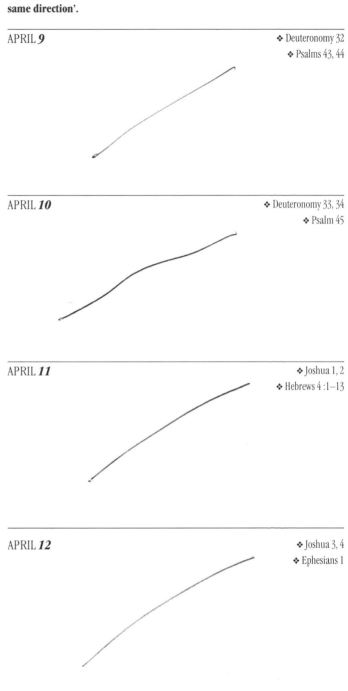

APRIL **13**
❖ Joshua 5, 6
❖ Ephesians 2

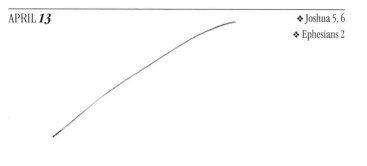

'God shifts us from one extreme to the other … This is meant to
ensure that we do not settle into any situation but remain
pliable, and to make us recognise that true insight does not come
from what we have grasped but from ever greater readiness and
deeper obedience.'

Hans Urs von Balthasar

APRIL **14**
❖ Joshua 7, 8
❖ Ephesians 3

APRIL **15**
❖ Joshua 9, 10
❖ Ephesians 4

Israel's victory is already under threat from her fascination with the gods of the new land.

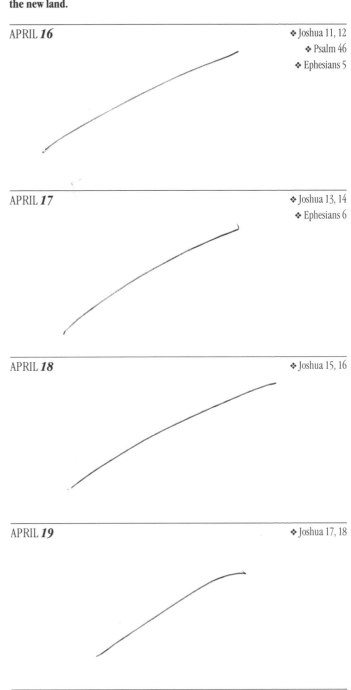

APRIL *16*

APRIL *17*

APRIL *18*

APRIL *19*

APRIL *20*

❖ Joshua 19, 20
❖ Psalm 47

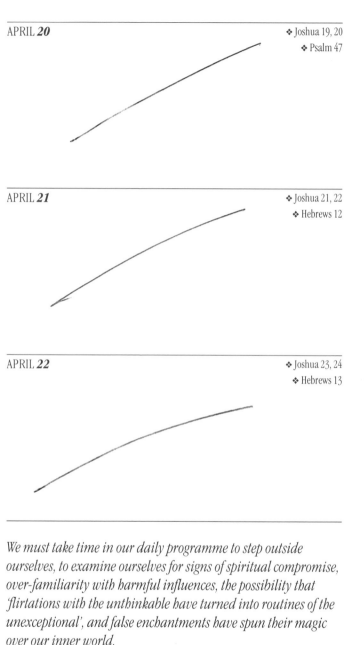

APRIL *21*

❖ Joshua 21, 22
❖ Hebrews 12

APRIL *22*

❖ Joshua 23, 24
❖ Hebrews 13

We must take time in our daily programme to step outside ourselves, to examine ourselves for signs of spiritual compromise, over-familiarity with harmful influences, the possibility that 'flirtations with the unthinkable have turned into routines of the unexceptional', and false enchantments have spun their magic over our inner world.

Israel is in cultural transition from her desert nomadic life to settled farming in Canaan. Her leaders, or 'Judges', are in crisis.

APRIL *23*

❖ Judges 1, 2
❖ 1 Corinthians 1

APRIL *24*

❖ Judges 3, 4
❖ Psalm 48
❖ 1 Corinthians 2

APRIL *25*

❖ Judges 5, 6
❖ 1 Corinthians 3

APRIL *26*

❖ Judges 7, 8
❖ 1 Corinthians 4

At Corinth, Christians are caught in chaotic transition from a life of paganism to a life of holiness within the body of Christ.

APRIL **27**
❖ Judges 9, 10
❖ 1 Corinthians 5

APRIL **28**
❖ Judges 11, 12
❖ 1 Corinthians 6

'If beauty delights you, "the dust shall shine as the sun". If you enjoy that speed, strength and freedom of the body that nothing can withstand, "they shall be like the angels of God" ... If you delight in any pleasure that is not impure but pure, "they shall drink from the torrent of the pleasure" of God.'

Anselm, eleventh century

APRIL **29**
❖ Judges 13, 14
❖ 1 Corinthians 7

Two clues to the quality of a culture: sex and idols.

APRIL *30*
❖ Judges 15
❖ 1 Corinthians 8
❖ Psalm 49

MAY *1*
❖ Judges 16, 17
❖ 1 Corinthians 9

MAY *2*
❖ Judges 18, 19
❖ Ruth 1, 2

MAY *3*
❖ Judges 20, 21
❖ Ruth 3, 4

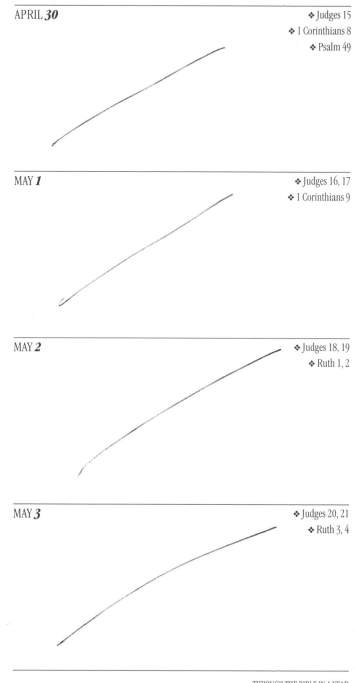

The Corinthians discover the secret of Christian living: love reigns wherever Jesus is Lord.

MAY **4**

❖ 1 Samuel 1, 2
❖ 1 Corinthians 10, 11

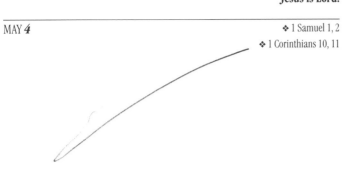

'The Christian style of life is marked by an extraordinary combination of detachment and concern. The Christian will care less for the world and, at the same time, care more for it than the person who is not a Christian. He will not lose his heart to it, but he may well lose his life for it.'

John Robinson

MAY **5**

❖ 1 Samuel 3, 4
❖ 1 Corinthians 12, 13

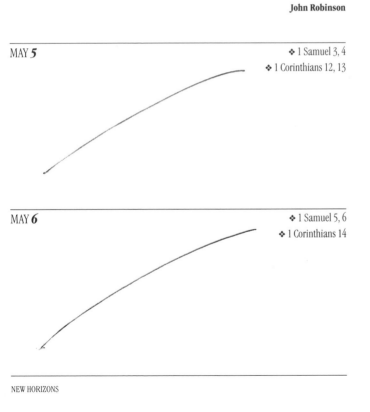

MAY **6**

❖ 1 Samuel 5, 6
❖ 1 Corinthians 14

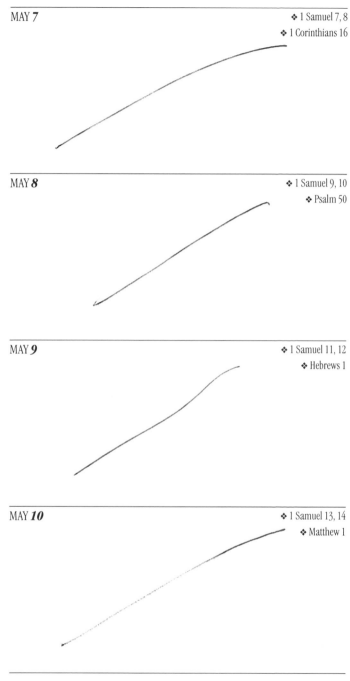

MAY **7**

❖ 1 Samuel 7, 8
❖ 1 Corinthians 16

MAY **8**

❖ 1 Samuel 9, 10
❖ Psalm 50

MAY **9**

❖ 1 Samuel 11, 12
❖ Hebrews 1

MAY **10**

❖ 1 Samuel 13, 14
❖ Matthew 1

WHERE IS THE KING?

King Saul thought Goliath was too big to fight: David thought he was too big to miss.

MAY **11**
❖ 1 Samuel 15, 16
❖ Matthew 2

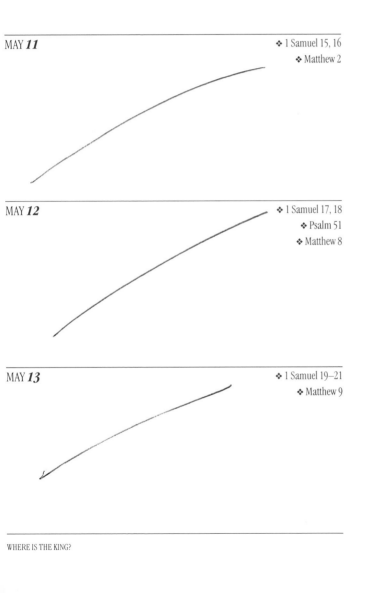

MAY **12**
❖ 1 Samuel 17, 18
❖ Psalm 51
❖ Matthew 8

MAY **13**
❖ 1 Samuel 19–21
❖ Matthew 9

WHERE IS THE KING?

David demonstrates the touch of divine kingship in the way he exercises justice, power and compassion.

| MAY **14** | ❖ 1 Samuel 22, 23 |
| | ❖ Matthew 10 |

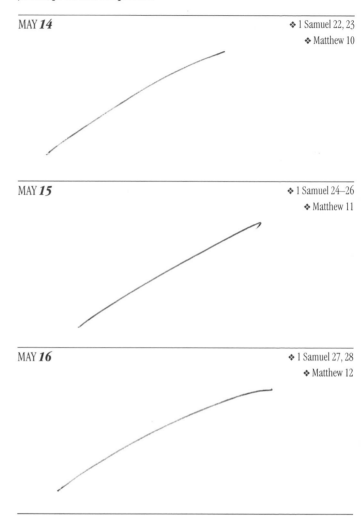

| MAY **15** | ❖ 1 Samuel 24–26 |
| | ❖ Matthew 11 |

| MAY **16** | ❖ 1 Samuel 27, 28 |
| | ❖ Matthew 12 |

'Christ lies in a manger, but he holds the world. He nurses at his mother's breast, but he feeds the angels. He is wrapped in swaddling clothes, but he gives us the garment of immortality ... that our weakness might be made strong, his strength has been made weak.'

Augustine of Hippo, fifth century

In Jesus, 'the kingdom of God has come upon you'.

MAY *17*

❖ 1 Samuel 29–31
❖ Matthew 13

MAY *18*

❖ 2 Samuel 1, 2
❖ Matthew 14

MAY *19*

❖ 2 Samuel 3–5
❖ Matthew 15

MAY *20*

❖ 2 Samuel 6, 7
❖ Matthew 16
Psalm 52

WHERE IS THE KING?

Israel will look back on David's reign as a golden time of faith and expansion.

MAY **21**

❖ 2 Samuel 8–10
❖ Matthew 17

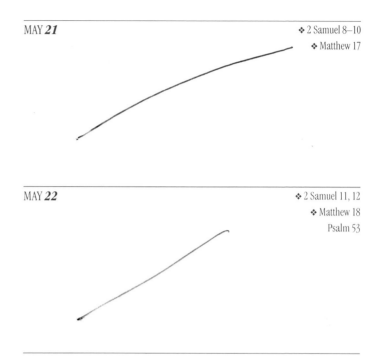

MAY **22**

❖ 2 Samuel 11, 12
❖ Matthew 18
Psalm 53

'Blessed are you, Sovereign God of all, to you be glory and praise forever! As we look for your coming among us this day, open our eyes to behold your presence, and strengthen our hands to do your will, that the world may rejoice and give you praise, Father, Son and Holy Spirit. Amen.'

From *Celebrating Common Prayer*

MAY **23**

❖ 2 Samuel 13, 14
❖ Matthew 19

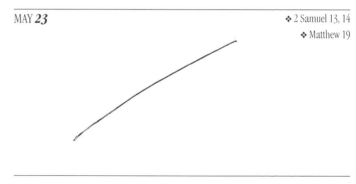

Jesus, 'great David's greater Son', established God's rule when he smashed Satan by his cross and resurrection.

MAY *24*	❖ 2 Samuel 15, 16
	❖ Matthew 20

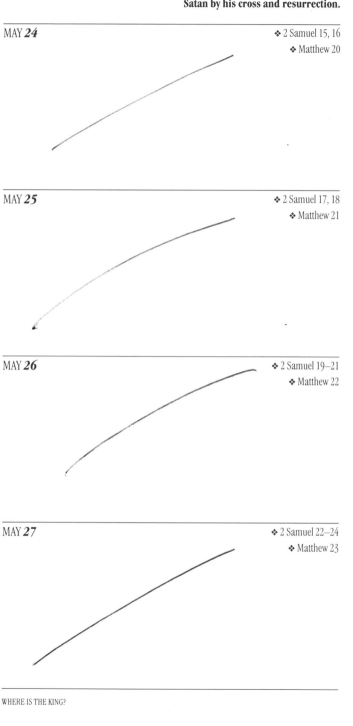

MAY *25*	❖ 2 Samuel 17, 18
	❖ Matthew 21

MAY *26*	❖ 2 Samuel 19–21
	❖ Matthew 22

MAY *27*	❖ 2 Samuel 22–24
	❖ Matthew 23

WHERE IS THE KING?

David and Solomon - flawed symbols of God's power and wisdom in government.

MAY **28**

❖ 1 Kings 1, 2
❖ Psalm 54

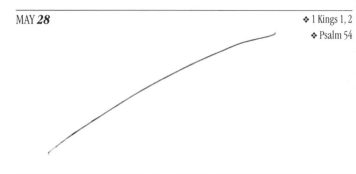

'The Celtic Church saw movement as the essence of the Gospel … they had a basic understanding that evangelism is linked with a thrust from an area of safety into a potentially dangerous world. Today's church often wants mission without movement, and it becomes no more than a polite request to the world to come and hear the Gospel. When the world just as politely declines, the church is nonplussed and wrings its hands over human obduracy.' **John Finney**

MAY **29**

❖ 1 Kings 3–5
❖ Matthew 25

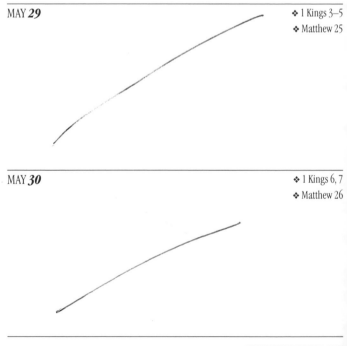

MAY **30**

❖ 1 Kings 6, 7
❖ Matthew 26

In Christ the King, the transfiguration of all creation is dawning.

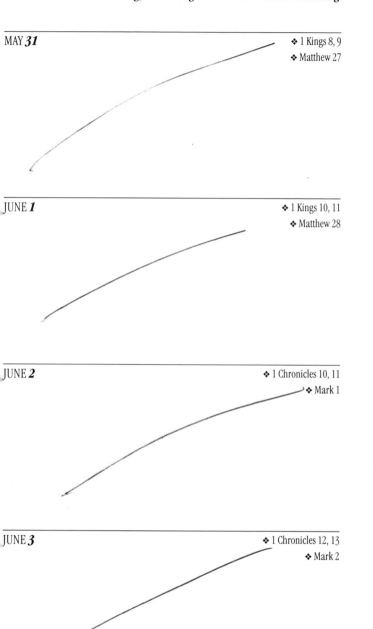

MAY **31**

❖ 1 Kings 8, 9
❖ Matthew 27

JUNE **1**

❖ 1 Kings 10, 11
❖ Matthew 28

JUNE **2**

❖ 1 Chronicles 10, 11
❖ Mark 1

JUNE **3**

❖ 1 Chronicles 12, 13
❖ Mark 2

WHERE IS THE KING?

Chronicles reinterprets Israel's history to show that the covenant community is 'a kingdom of priests and a holy nation'.

JUNE **4** ❖ 1 Chronicles 14, 15
❖ Mark 3

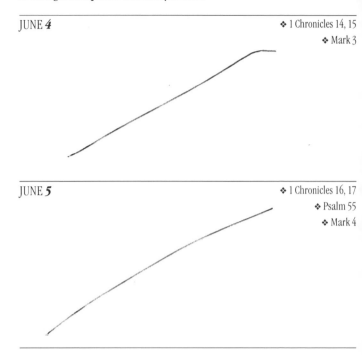

JUNE **5** ❖ 1 Chronicles 16, 17
❖ Psalm 55
❖ Mark 4

When we pray by the Holy Spirit, we participate in Christ's prayer.

*'In Meztich people were said to be like Shofarot, or rams horns!
Just as Shofarot can make no sound unless breath is blown
through, so too people can only say prayers because God moves
within them. When we pray, we choose to be a vessel for words
that flow through all creation, with or without our consent.'*

Lawrence Kushner

JUNE **6** ❖ 1 Chronicles 18, 19
❖ Mark 5

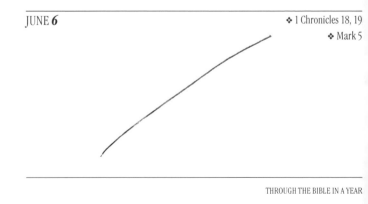

Mark's account of the good news of Jesus provides rich material for the missionary church.

| JUNE **7** | ❖ 1 Chronicles 20, 21 |
| | ❖ Mark 6 |

| JUNE **8** | ❖ 1 Chronicles 22, 23 |
| | ❖ Mark 7 |

| JUNE **9** | ❖ 1 Chronicles 24—27 |
| | ❖ Mark 8 |

| JUNE **10** | ❖ 1 Chronicles 28, 29 |
| | ❖ Mark 9 |

The Chronicler sees the worshipping community gathering in the holy city of Jerusalem.

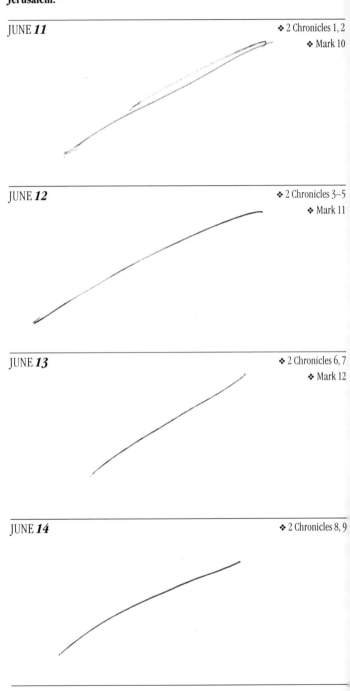

JUNE *11*

❖ 2 Chronicles 1, 2
❖ Mark 10

JUNE *12*

❖ 2 Chronicles 3–5
❖ Mark 11

JUNE *13*

❖ 2 Chronicles 6, 7
❖ Mark 12

JUNE *14*

❖ 2 Chronicles 8, 9

Mark concludes with the risen Lord Jesus sending his disciples out of Jerusalem 'into all the world'.

JUNE **15**

❖ 2 Chronicles 10–12
❖ Mark 14

JUNE **16**

❖ 2 Chronicles 13–15
❖ Mark 15

JUNE **17**

❖ 2 Chronicles 16, 17
❖ Mark 16

Lord, I will mean and speak thy praise, thy praise alone.
... Wherefore I sing. Yet since my heart, though pressed, runs thin;
O that I might some other hearts convert,
And so take up at use good store:
That to thy chests there might be coming in
Both all my praise, and more!

George Herbert, 'Praise III'

Faith and culture in conflict.

JUNE *18*   ❖ 2 Chronicles 18–20
     ❖ Ecclesiastes 1

JUNE *19*   ❖ 2 Chronicles 21–23
     ❖ Ecclesiastes 2

JUNE *20*   ❖ 2 Chronicles 24, 25
     ❖ Ecclesiastes 3

JUNE *21*   ❖ 2 Chronicles 26–28
     ❖ Ecclesiastes 4

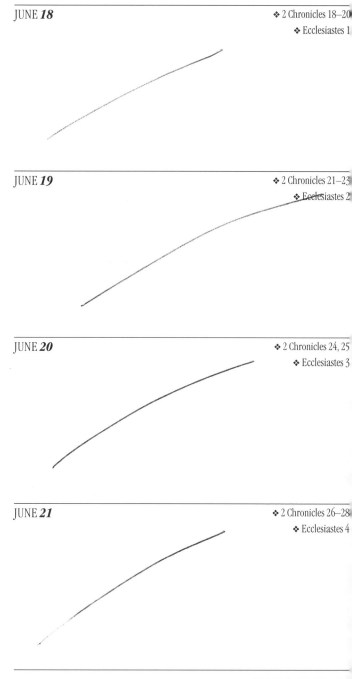

A compromising, accomodating church will never challenge the cultures.

JUNE **22**

❖ 2 Chronicles 29, 30
❖ Ecclesiastes 5

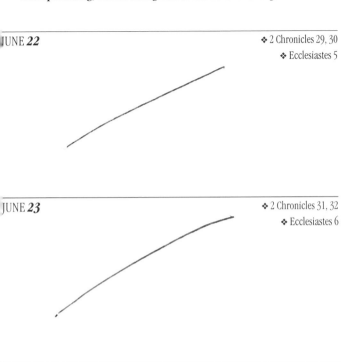

JUNE **23**

❖ 2 Chronicles 31, 32
❖ Ecclesiastes 6

'Man is an exception, whatever else he is. If it is not true that a divine being fell, then we can only say that one of the animals went entirely off its head.' **G K Chesterton**

'Man is the only animal that laughs and weeps; for he is the only animal that is struck by the difference between what things are and what they might have been.' **William Hazlitt**

JUNE **24**

❖ 2 Chronicles 33, 34
❖ Ecclesiastes 7

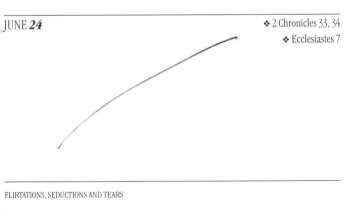

In Ecclesiastes, a believer is trying to put himself into the mind of the humanist or secularist.

JUNE *25*

❖ 2 Chronicles 35, 36
❖ Ecclesiastes 8

JUNE *26*

❖ 1 Kings 12, 13
❖ Ecclesiastes 9

JUNE *27*

❖ 1 Kings 14, 15
❖ Ecclesiastes 10

JUNE *28*

❖ 1 Kings 16, 17
❖ Ecclesiastes 11
❖ Psalm 56

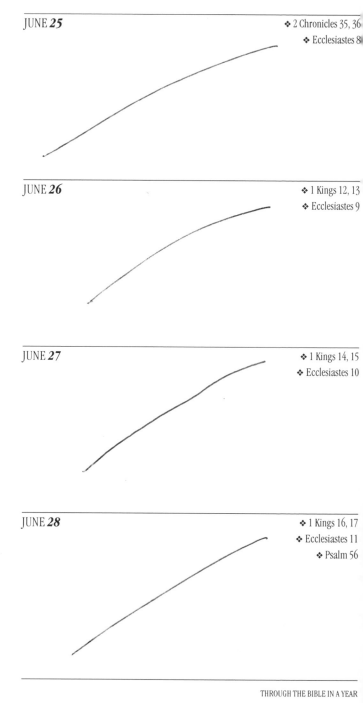

The prophet is the conscience of the covenant people.

JUNE **29**

❖ 1 Kings 18, 19
❖ Ecclesiastes 12
❖ Psalm 57

*The contemporary Christian is compelled to live within a culture
of unbelief which says, 'Worship if you want; pray if you must.
But whatever you do, do not on any account take your religion
seriously, as if it makes any real difference.' Seriousness in faith
is the unforgivable sin against the spirit of modern secularism.*

JUNE **30**

❖ 1 Kings 20, 21
❖Psalm 58

JULY **1**

❖ 1 Kings 22
❖ Psalms 59, 60

FLIRTATIONS, SEDUCTIONS AND TEARS

Where is Christ at this moment? Walking among his embattled people.

JULY *2*

❖ 2 Kings 1, 2
❖ Revelation 1

JULY *3*

❖ 2 Kings 3, 4
❖ Revelation 2

JULY *4*

❖ 2 Kings 5, 6
❖ Revelation 3

JULY *5*

❖ 2 Kings 7, 8

Through Elisha, God addresses the political chaos that is threatening Israel.

The believer has safety in depth. Only a deep, thoughtful, reflective communion with God will save us from yielding to cultural seductions.

'Thanksgiving begins in the moment in which I see my own existence as giftedness. Nicholas of Cusa prayed "How could you give yourself to me if you had not first given me to myself?" Gabriel Marcel wrote "Everything is gift. The receiver of the gift is himself the first gift received." '

John O'Donnell SJ

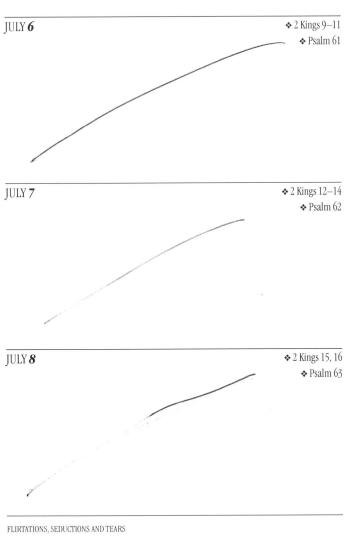

JULY **6**
❖ 2 Kings 9–11
❖ Psalm 61

JULY **7**
❖ 2 Kings 12–14
❖ Psalm 62

JULY **8**
❖ 2 Kings 15, 16
❖ Psalm 63

Jerusalem, ruined by the acids of compromise.

JULY **9**   ❖ 2 Kings 17, 18
                                                                                   ❖ Psalm 64

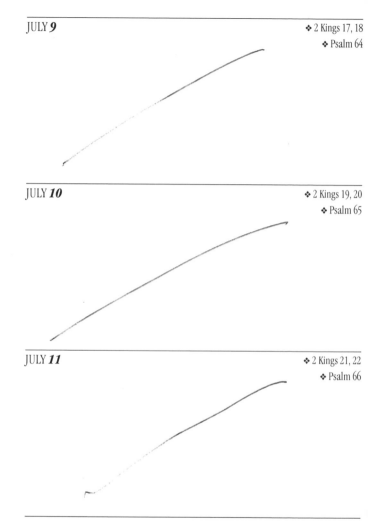

JULY **10**   ❖ 2 Kings 19, 20
                                                                                   ❖ Psalm 65

JULY **11**   ❖ 2 Kings 21, 22
                                                                                   ❖ Psalm 66

'In the prophetic religion of the Bible, human decisions and actions become the sources of surprise. Each discrete act is our response to the God of history. Our actions have profound and unrepeatable significance. Reading the morning paper becomes a religious act, for it sets the agenda of what must be repaired this day.'

Lawrence Kushner

JULY **12**   ❖ 2 Kings 23–25

JULY **13**   ❖ Amos 1–3

JULY **14**   ❖ Amos 4–6

JULY **15**   ❖ Amos 7–9

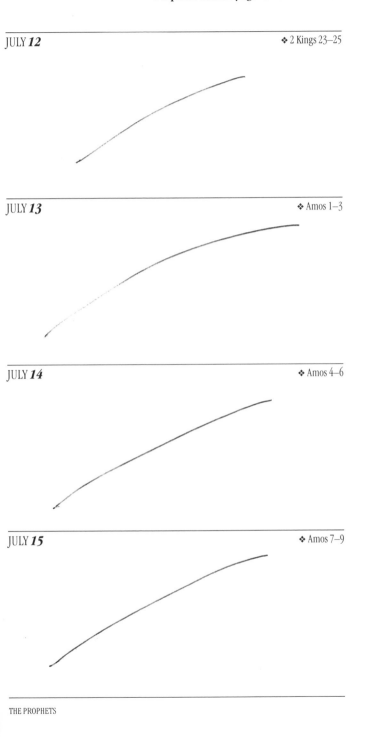

THE PROPHETS

Pleading, nagging, wooing: the prophet enacts God's seeking love.

JULY **16** ❖ Hosea 1–3

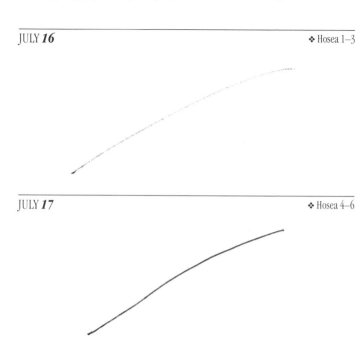

JULY **17** ❖ Hosea 4–6

'The heights of heaven cannot contain your presence, yet you have a dwelling in my mind. I try to conceal your glorious name in my heart, but my desire for you grows till it bursts out of my mouth. Therefore I shall praise the name of the Lord as long as the breath of the living God is in my nostrils.'

Solomon Ibn Gabriol, eleventh century

JULY **18** ❖ Hosea 7–9

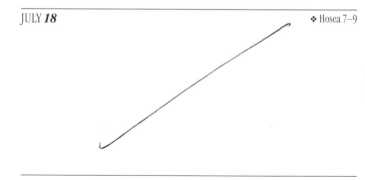

The prophet is unable to remain quiet about his experiences. He must proclaim what God reveals.

JULY *19* ❖ Hosea 10–12

JULY *20* ❖ Hosea 13, 14
Psalm 67

JULY *21* ❖ Jonah 1–4

JULY *22* ❖ Micah 1–3

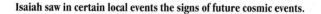

JULY **23**

❖ Micah 4, 5
❖ Psalm 68

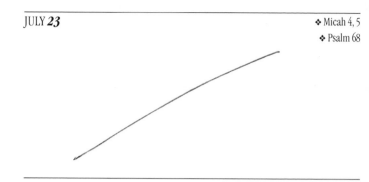

'When a composer such as God creates the opera of the world and places in its centre his crucified and risen Son, every fault-finding at his work – ie whether or not he could have done it better – must be reduced to silence.'

Hans Urs von Balthasar

JULY **24**

❖ Micah 6, 7
❖ Psalm 69

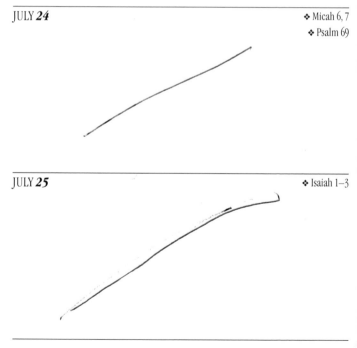

JULY **25**

❖ Isaiah 1–3

The prophets discerned the hand of God inside the glove of history.

JULY **26**	❖ Isaiah 4–6

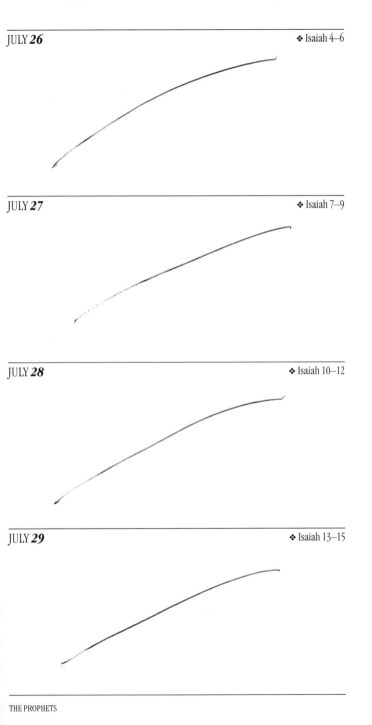

JULY **27**	❖ Isaiah 7–9

JULY **28**	❖ Isaiah 10–12

JULY **29**	❖ Isaiah 13–15

God persuades the ambitions of the nations to serve his purposes.

On the old Irish hymn – 'Be thou my vision' – Irish scholar Terence McCaughey comments that the word translated 'vision' actually indicates 'the heightened awareness of those who are possessed by battle frenzy, becoming berserk'. We are asking, therefore, for a furious love, a rage for love, justice, healing, goodness, peace, and for the high glory of God, in the daily battle of faith.

JULY **30** ❖ Isaiah 16–18

JULY **31** ❖ Isaiah 19–21

AUGUST **1** ❖ Isaiah 22–24

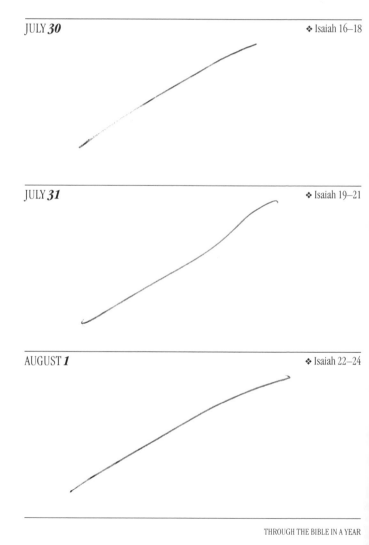

Like a potter at his wheel, God works with the clay of international mayhem.

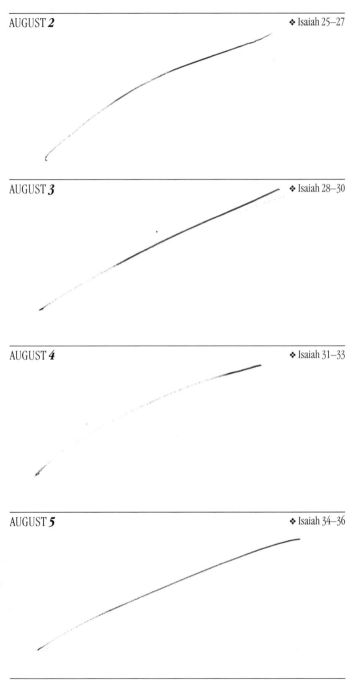

AUGUST *2* ❖ Isaiah 25–27

AUGUST *3* ❖ Isaiah 28–30

AUGUST *4* ❖ Isaiah 31–33

AUGUST *5* ❖ Isaiah 34–36

THE PROPHETS

Where is God? The prophets say that he is in the thick of the action.

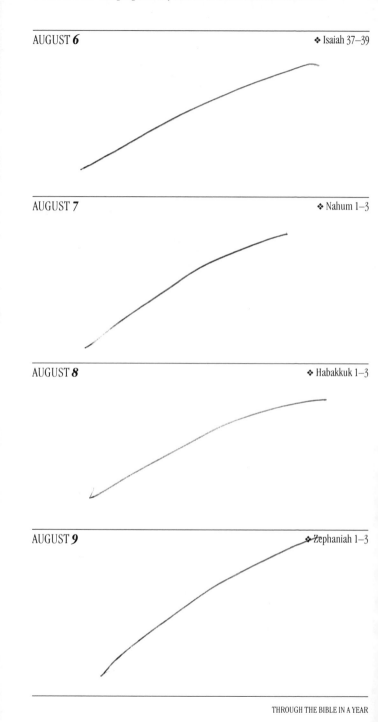

AUGUST **6**   ❖ Isaiah 37–39

AUGUST **7**   ❖ Nahum 1–3

AUGUST **8**   ❖ Habakkuk 1–3

AUGUST **9**   ❖ Zephaniah 1–3

Jeremiah lays bare the inner turmoil of a man singled out to speak to God.

AUGUST **10** ❖ Jeremiah 1–3

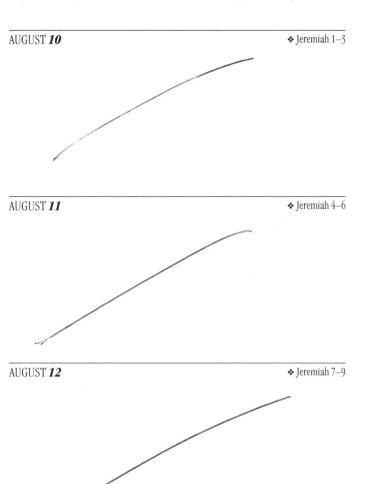

AUGUST **11** ❖ Jeremiah 4–6

AUGUST **12** ❖ Jeremiah 7–9

Jeremiah, as indeed every believer should, trafficked between God and people.

'There is a chamber in God himself, into which none can enter but the one, the individual, the peculiar man – out of which chamber that man has to bring revelation and strength for his brethren. This is that for which he was made – to reveal the secret things of the Father.' **George MacDonald**

The overpowering urge of God's word within impels Jeremiah into his ministry.

AUGUST *13*   ❖ Jeremiah 10–12

AUGUST *14*   ❖ Jeremiah 13–15

AUGUST *15*   ❖ Jeremiah 16–18

AUGUST *16*   ❖ Jeremiah 19–21

AUGUST *17* ❖ Jeremiah 22–24

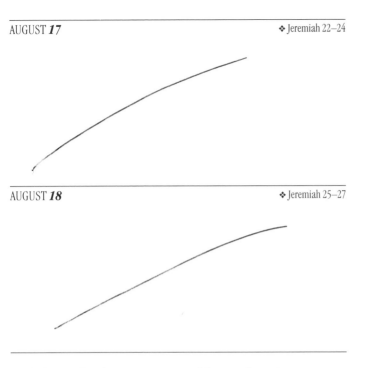

AUGUST *18* ❖ Jeremiah 25–27

At the heart of God's engagement with his people is always one and the same question: 'Do you love me?' Love is the only service that power cannot command nor money buy. Duty makes us do things well, but love makes us do them beautifully.

'What does it mean to love God? To strain one's soul continually, beyond one's powers, toward the will of God, with the goal and desire of giving him honour.' **Bishop Basil, fourth century**

AUGUST *19* ❖ Jeremiah 28–30

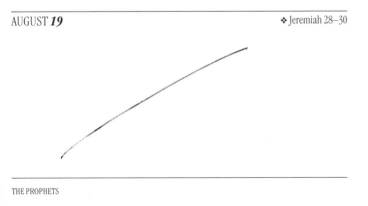

Blind and stubborn, Israel rejects Jeremiah's warnings and is taken into captivity in Babylon.

AUGUST *20*   ❖ Jeremiah 31–33

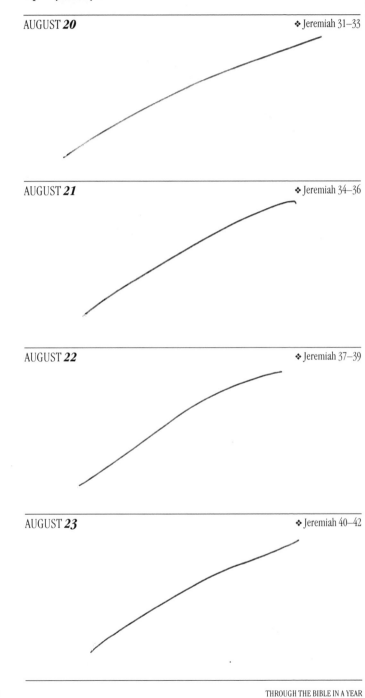

AUGUST *21*   ❖ Jeremiah 34–36

AUGUST *22*   ❖ Jeremiah 37–39

AUGUST *23*   ❖ Jeremiah 40–42

Even in exile, Israel can depend upon God's unbreakable covenant love.

AUGUST *24*   ❖ Jeremiah 43–45

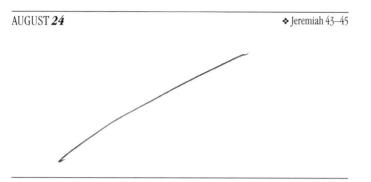

But how, we ask, can the God of all love 'punish' his people?

'The fire of God, which is his essential being, his love, his creative power, is fire unlike its earthly symbol in this, that it is only at a distance that it burns; that the further from him, it burns the worse.'

George MacDonald

AUGUST *25*   ❖ Jeremiah 46–48

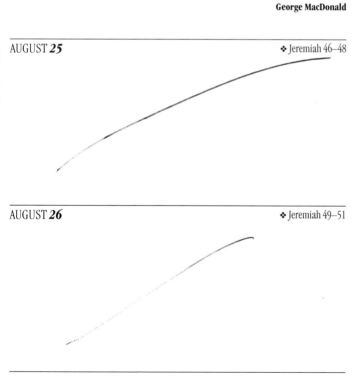

AUGUST *26*   ❖ Jeremiah 49–51

What is left when the glory departs from the temple?

AUGUST *27* ❖ Jeremiah 52
❖ Psalm 70

AUGUST *28* ❖ Lamentations 1, 2
❖ Psalm 71

AUGUST *29* ❖ Lamentations 3–5

AUGUST *30* ❖ Ezekiel 1–3

How brittle are the Piers
On which our Faith doth tread –
No Bridge below doth totter so –
Yet none hath such a Crowd.

It is as old as God –
Indeed – 'twas built by him –
He sent his Son to test the Plank,
And he pronounced it firm.

Emily Dickinson, 'Poem 1433'

AUGUST**31** ❖ Ezekiel 4–6

SEPTEMBER **1** ❖ Ezekiel 7–9

SEPTEMBER **2** ❖ Ezekiel 10–12

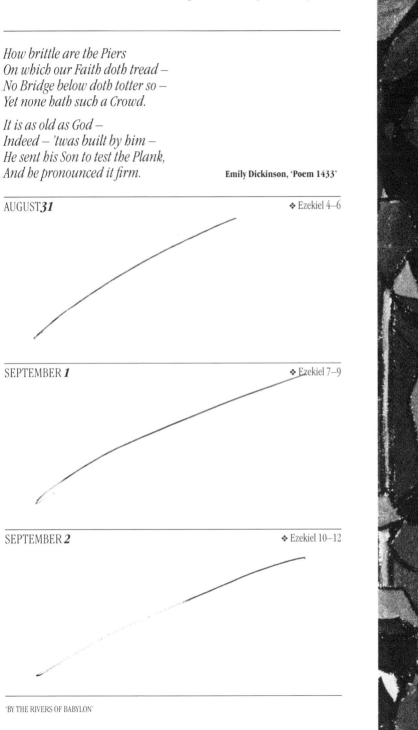

'BY THE RIVERS OF BABYLON'

Ezekiel's diagnosis? These people were never in love with their Lord in the first place.

SEPTEMBER *3* ❖Ezekiel 13–15

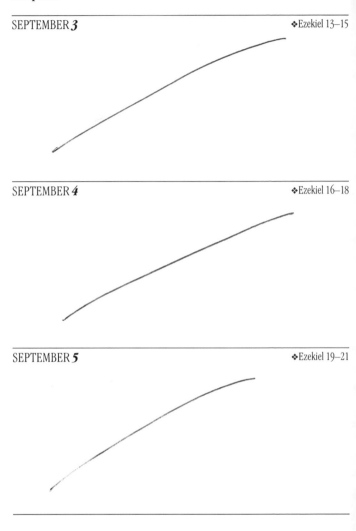

SEPTEMBER *4* ❖Ezekiel 16–18

SEPTEMBER *5* ❖Ezekiel 19–21

'I called to the Lord from my prison – and he answered me in the freedom of space.'

Victor Frankel, on his experience in the concentration camps

Jerusalem has fallen, but Israel will be healed through the discipline of captivity.

SEPTEMBER *6*

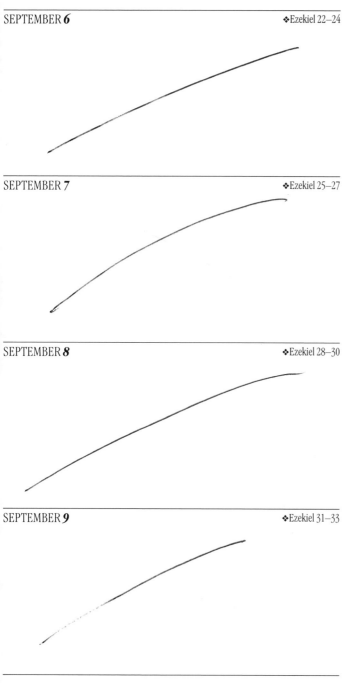

❖Ezekiel 22–24

SEPTEMBER 7

❖Ezekiel 25–27

SEPTEMBER *8*

❖Ezekiel 28–30

SEPTEMBER *9*

❖Ezekiel 31–33

The valley of bones and the river of life are visions of the covenant renewed in the Holy Spirit – the 'new covenant'.

SEPTEMBER **10**   ❖ Ezekiel 34–36

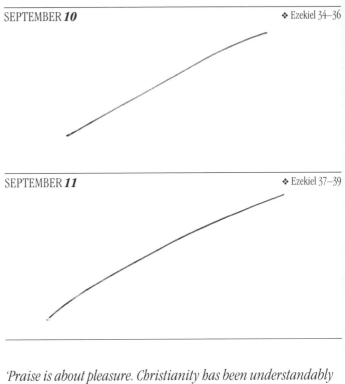

SEPTEMBER **11**   ❖ Ezekiel 37–39

'Praise is about pleasure. Christianity has been understandably reticent about the joy, bliss, delight and sheer pleasure at its heart. But it is so, simply because its God is the God of joy. Christian hedonism is the holy intoxication of pleasing and being pleased by God, and that sums up the experience of true praise.'

David Ford

SEPTEMBER **12**   ❖ Ezekiel 40–42

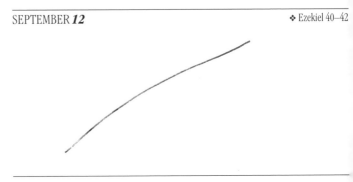

Daniel is God's man in the midst of the nation's suffering. Job is God's man in the mystery of personal suffering.

| SEPTEMBER *13* | ❖ Ezekiel 43–45 |

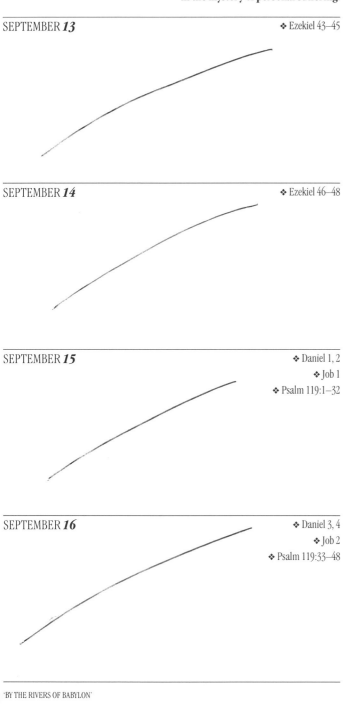

| SEPTEMBER *14* | ❖ Ezekiel 46–48 |

SEPTEMBER *15*	❖ Daniel 1, 2
	❖ Job 1
	❖ Psalm 119:1–32

SEPTEMBER *16*	❖ Daniel 3, 4
	❖ Job 2
	❖ Psalm 119:33–48

'BY THE RIVERS OF BABYLON'

Daniel's vision of Christ among the cosmic powers.

SEPTEMBER *17*
❖ Daniel 5, 6
❖ Job 3
❖ Psalm 119:49–72

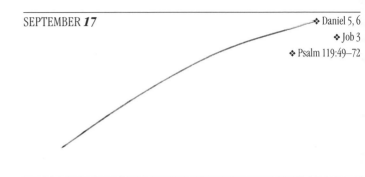

'In the same way that God's presence can be anywhere and any time, so too any act may be historic. One vote can change the result of an election, a joke at the right moment can change the course of a meeting, anywhere and any time the most otherwise trivial gesture can and does have world-historic consequences. But we rarely realise the effect until too late. It is incumbent upon us to remember that each moment can be decisive and therefore historic.' **Lawrence Kushner**

SEPTEMBER *18*
❖ Daniel 7, 8
❖ Job 4

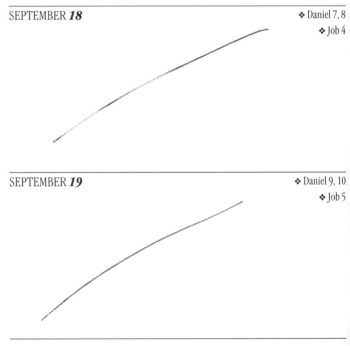

SEPTEMBER *19*
❖ Daniel 9, 10
❖ Job 5

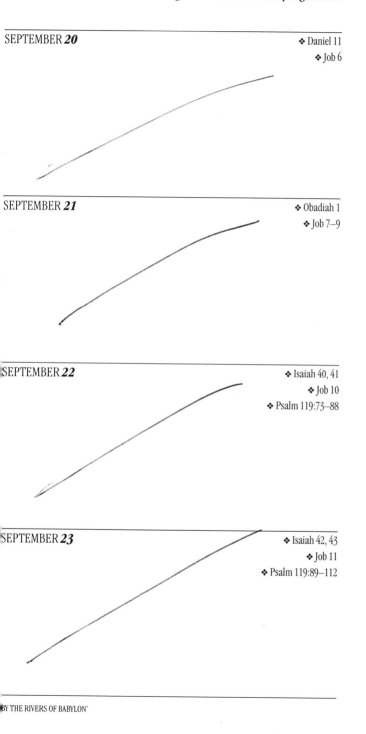

SEPTEMBER *20*

❖ Daniel 11
❖ Job 6

SEPTEMBER *21*

❖ Obadiah 1
❖ Job 7–9

SEPTEMBER *22*

❖ Isaiah 40, 41
❖ Job 10
❖ Psalm 119:73–88

SEPTEMBER *23*

❖ Isaiah 42, 43
❖ Job 11
❖ Psalm 119:89–112

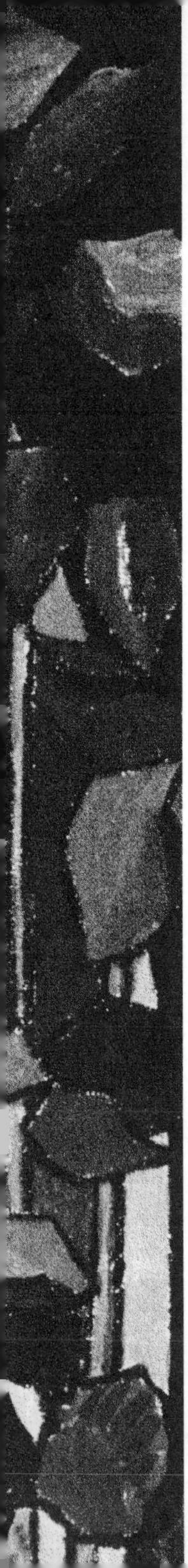

Exiles must beware of assimilation. Don't let Babylon inside your head.

Thou mastering me
God! giver of breath and bread;
World's strand, sway of the sea;
Lord of living and dead;
Thou has bound bones and veins in me, fastened me flesh.
And after it almost unmade, what with dread,
Thy doing: and dost thou touch me afresh?
Over again I feel thy finger and find thee.

Gerard Manley Hopkins
'The Wreck of the Deutschland'

SEPTEMBER *24*

❖ Isaiah 44, 45
❖ Job 12
❖ Psalm 119:113–144

SEPTEMBER *25*

❖ Isaiah 46, 47
❖ Job 13

SEPTEMBER *26*

❖ Isaiah 48, 49
❖ Job 14

God doesn't answer Job's problem of innocent suffering, but the problem is becoming more luminous.

SEPTEMBER **27**

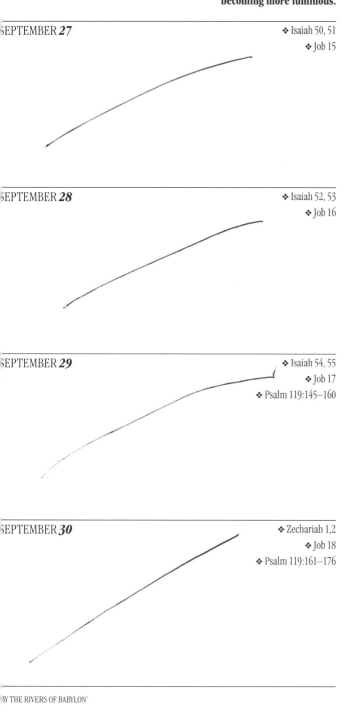

SEPTEMBER **28**

SEPTEMBER **29**

SEPTEMBER **30**

A restored people, a renewed worship, an invitation to the nations.

OCTOBER *1*

❖ Zechariah 3, 4
❖ Job 19

OCTOBER *2*

❖ Zechariah 5, 6
❖ Job 20

OCTOBER *3*

❖ Zechariah 7, 8
❖ Job 21

OCTOBER *4*

❖ Zechariah 9, 10
❖ Job 22

Zechariah's vision: all the nations will come and celebrate God's feast.

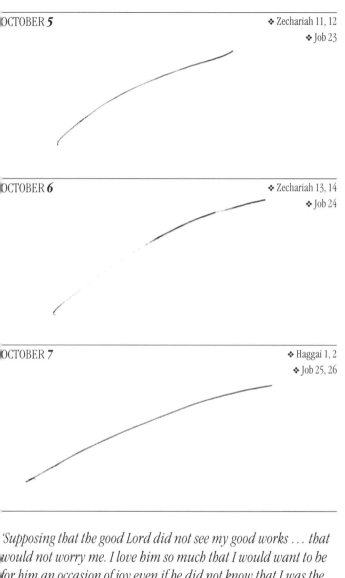

OCTOBER **5**
❖ Zechariah 11, 12
❖ Job 23

OCTOBER **6**
❖ Zechariah 13, 14
❖ Job 24

OCTOBER **7**
❖ Haggai 1, 2
❖ Job 25, 26

'Supposing that the good Lord did not see my good works ... that would not worry me. I love him so much that I would want to be for him an occasion of joy even if he did not know that I was the one responsible. Once he knows it and sees it, then he is obliged, so to speak, to reward me. And I would like to spare him this effort.'

Thérèse of Lisieux

Visions of God breaking in on 'the Day of the Lord'.

OCTOBER **8**

❖ Joel 1–
❖ Psalm 72

OCTOBER **9**

❖ Malachi 1, 2
❖ Job 27

OCTOBER **10**

❖ Malachi 3, 4
❖ Job 28

OCTOBER **11**

❖ Ezra 1, 2
❖ Job 29, 30

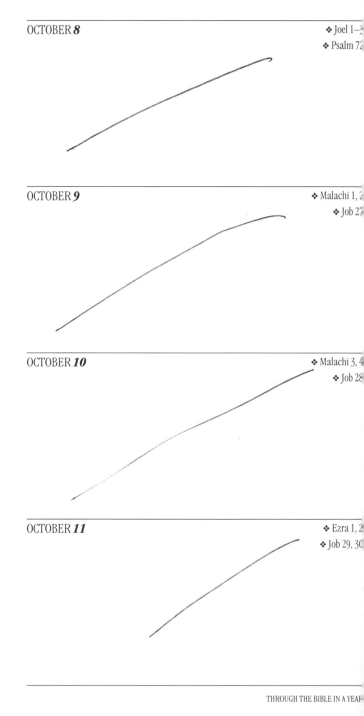

New worshippers, new worship. The returning exiles rebuild the temple in Jerusalem.

OCTOBER **12**

❖ Ezra 3, 4
❖ Job 31, 32

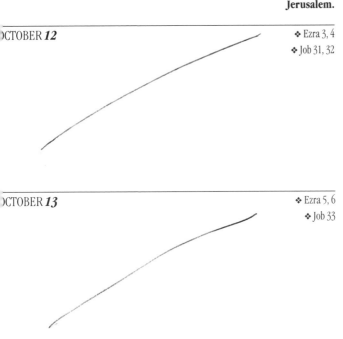

OCTOBER **13**

❖ Ezra 5, 6
❖ Job 33

The Christian's task is to point to where the Spirit of Christ is revealed, where there is evidence of the kingdom, where the rule of God is made plain in the world.

'The Christian knows what the world does not know, that it is by the power of God that Satan exists, by his permission that he rebels, and by his will that the kingdom of Messiah subdues him.'

Austin Farrer

OCTOBER **14**

❖ Ezra 7, 8
❖ Job 34

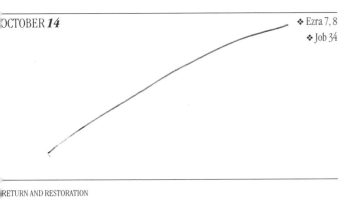

Restoration is a fight every inch of the way.

OCTOBER **15**

❖ Ezra 9, 1●
❖ Job 35, 3●

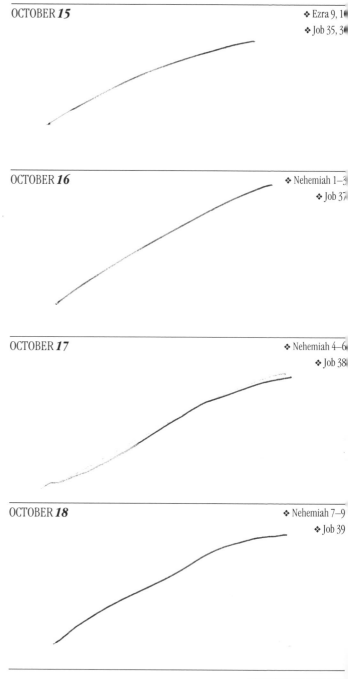

OCTOBER **16**

❖ Nehemiah 1–3●
❖ Job 37●

OCTOBER **17**

❖ Nehemiah 4–6●
❖ Job 38●

OCTOBER **18**

❖ Nehemiah 7–9
❖ Job 39

Face to face with God, Job realises that God is himself the 'answer' to the mystery of innocent suffering.

OCTOBER **19**

❖ Nehemiah 10, 11
❖ Job 40, 41

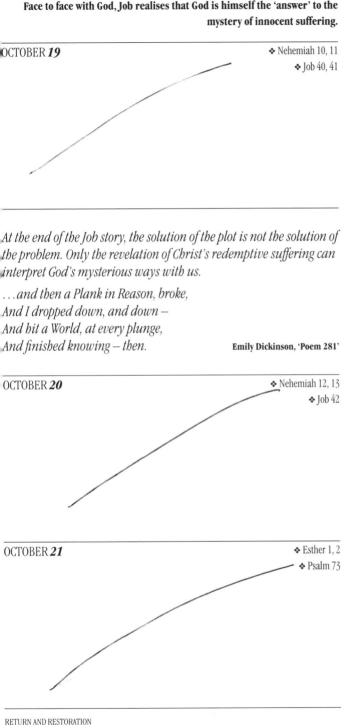

At the end of the Job story, the solution of the plot is not the solution of the problem. Only the revelation of Christ's redemptive suffering can interpret God's mysterious ways with us.

...and then a Plank in Reason, broke,
And I dropped down, and down –
And hit a World, at every plunge,
And finished knowing – then.
                                                          Emily Dickinson, 'Poem 281'

OCTOBER **20**

❖ Nehemiah 12, 13
❖ Job 42

OCTOBER **21**

❖ Esther 1, 2
❖ Psalm 73

RETURN AND RESTORATION

Anti-Semitism, ethnic cleansing: old hatreds foiled in Persia.

OCTOBER *22*

❖ Esther 3, 4
❖ Psalm 74

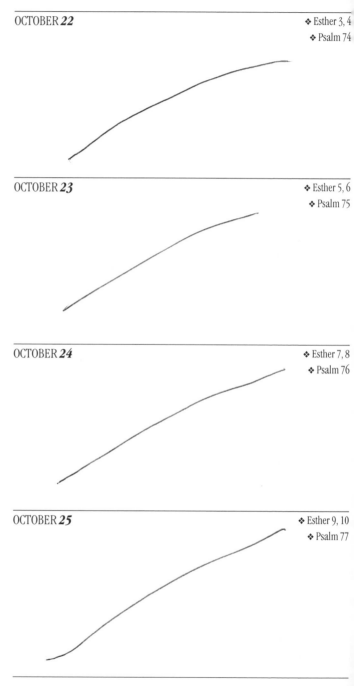

OCTOBER *23*

❖ Esther 5, 6
❖ Psalm 75

OCTOBER *24*

❖ Esther 7, 8
❖ Psalm 76

OCTOBER *25*

❖ Esther 9, 10
❖ Psalm 77

'The best way of thanking God is to taste his goodness with all our palate. It is no use making speeches of thanks to a musician if you are bored by his performance. You may deceive him, indeed, if you are a clever hypocrite, and can act the attention you can't be bothered to bestow. But God reads our hearts, and he knows whether we taste his kindness, or not. Enjoyment is the sincerest thanks.'
Austin Farrer

OCTOBER **26**
❖ Psalms 78–80
❖ Proverbs 1

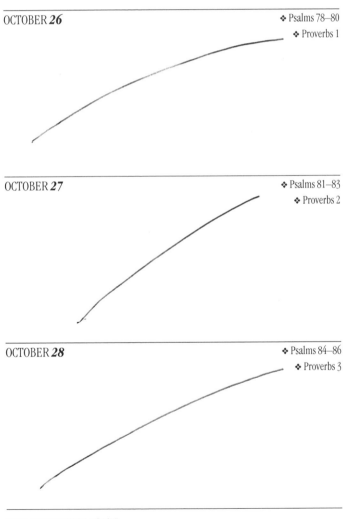

OCTOBER **27**
❖ Psalms 81–83
❖ Proverbs 2

OCTOBER **28**
❖ Psalms 84–86
❖ Proverbs 3

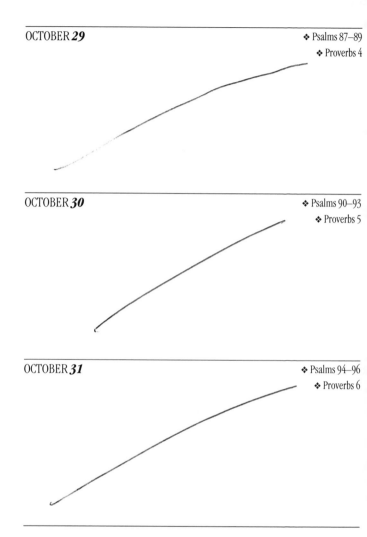

OCTOBER *29* ❖ Psalms 87–89
❖ Proverbs 4

OCTOBER *30* ❖ Psalms 90–93
❖ Proverbs 5

OCTOBER *31* ❖ Psalms 94–96
❖ Proverbs 6

'The Gospel is that all sin, evil and suffering, all need and want, can now be seen in the perspective of the resurrection of Jesus Christ in which God acts in such a way that the realistic response is joy … it is the joy of love between us and God, the ultimate mutuality and intimacy. That is why the Song of Songs is the best expression of the communication that flows from it.'

Daniel Hardy

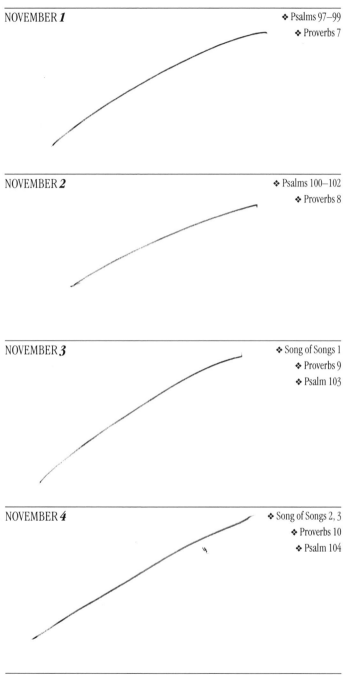

NOVEMBER *1*

❖ Psalms 97–99
❖ Proverbs 7

NOVEMBER *2*

❖ Psalms 100–102
❖ Proverbs 8

NOVEMBER *3*

❖ Song of Songs 1
❖ Proverbs 9
❖ Psalm 103

NOVEMBER *4*

❖ Song of Songs 2, 3
❖ Proverbs 10
❖ Psalm 104

'Who tastes thy goodness hunger still – who drinks thee cannot drink their fill.'

NOVEMBER **5**   ❖ Song of Songs 4, 5
                                                  ❖ Proverbs 11
                                                  ❖ Psalm 105

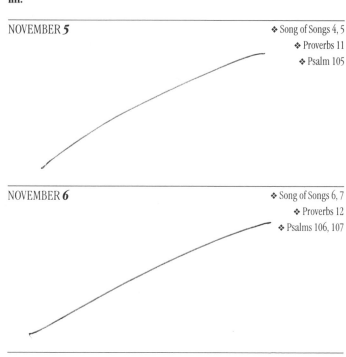

NOVEMBER **6**   ❖ Song of Songs 6, 7
                                                  ❖ Proverbs 12
                                                  ❖ Psalms 106, 107

'In my soul Christ seeks the will of the Father, and the Father seeks the image of the Son; when both of them meet there, my soul is full of the Holy Spirit.'

Hans Urs von Balthasar

NOVEMBER **7**   ❖ Song of Songs 8
                                                  ❖ Proverbs 13
                                                  ❖ Psalms 108–110

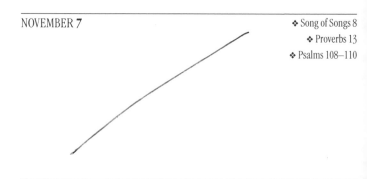

The story of redemption flows towards Jesus, and radiates from him.

NOVEMBER **8**

❖ Psalms 111–113
❖ Proverbs 14

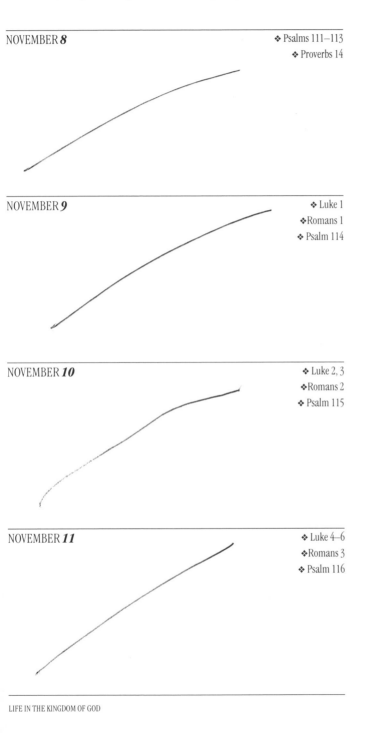

NOVEMBER **9**

❖ Luke 1
❖ Romans 1
❖ Psalm 114

NOVEMBER **10**

❖ Luke 2, 3
❖ Romans 2
❖ Psalm 115

NOVEMBER **11**

❖ Luke 4–6
❖ Romans 3
❖ Psalm 116

LIFE IN THE KINGDOM OF GOD

Jesus works his revolution in lives, ideas, ambitions.

NOVEMBER *12*

❖ Luke 7, 8
❖ Romans 5
❖ Psalm 117

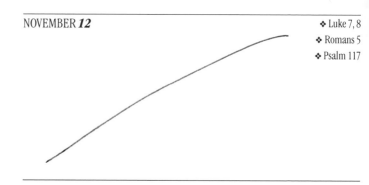

'If a person thinks that what he drinks should benefit only himself, then no living water will spring forth from him. But if he hastens to bring help to his neighbour, then his well spring does not dry up, because it is intent on flowing.'

Augustine of Hippo

NOVEMBER *13*

❖ Luke 9, 10
❖ Romans 6
❖ Psalm 118

NOVEMBER *14*

❖ Luke 11, 12
❖ Romans 7

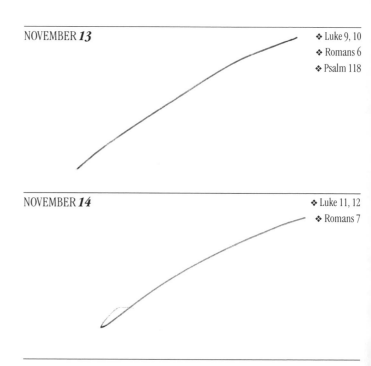

The Epistles interpret and apply the Gospels.

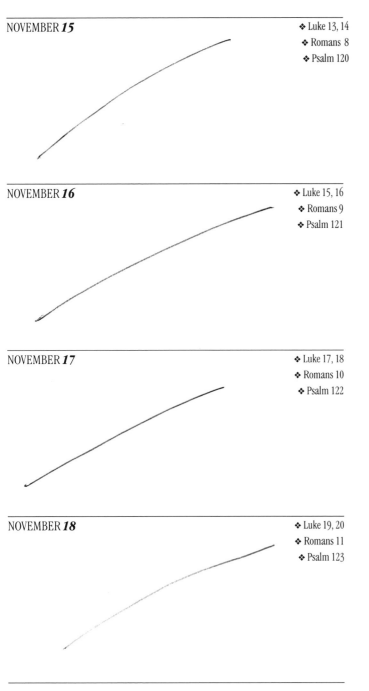

NOVEMBER **15**

❖ Luke 13, 14
❖ Romans 8
❖ Psalm 120

NOVEMBER **16**

❖ Luke 15, 16
❖ Romans 9
❖ Psalm 121

NOVEMBER **17**

❖ Luke 17, 18
❖ Romans 10
❖ Psalm 122

NOVEMBER **18**

❖ Luke 19, 20
❖ Romans 11
❖ Psalm 123

Christians confess that they are born again out of the miracle of Christ's cross and resurrection.

'What manners! To receive God's daily visit not in the living room of one's soul but in the kitchen or the hallway!'

Hans Urs von Balthasar

NOVEMBER *19*

❖ Luke 21, 22
❖ Romans 12
❖ Psalm 124

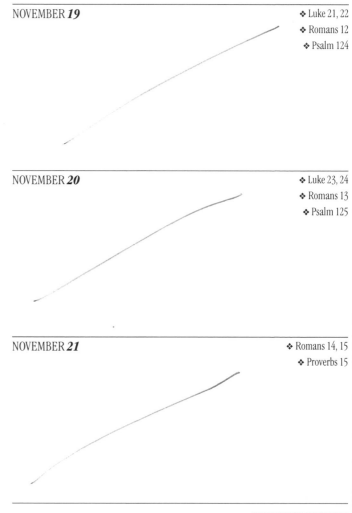

NOVEMBER *20*

❖ Luke 23, 24
❖ Romans 13
❖ Psalm 125

NOVEMBER *21*

❖ Romans 14, 15
❖ Proverbs 15

The new life we have in Jesus must be worked into the texture of each day's experiences.

NOVEMBER *22*
❖ Romans 16
❖ 2 Corinthians 1, 2

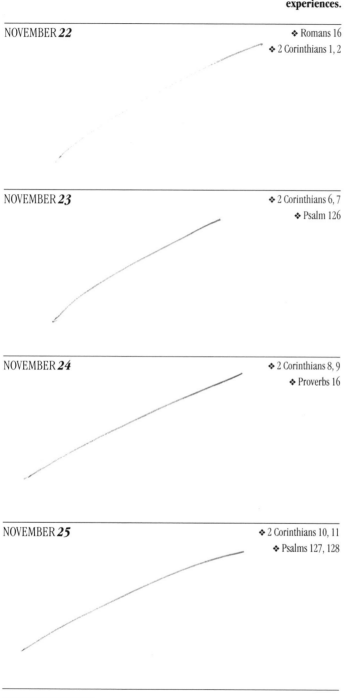

NOVEMBER *23*
❖ 2 Corinthians 6, 7
❖ Psalm 126

NOVEMBER *24*
❖ 2 Corinthians 8, 9
❖ Proverbs 16

NOVEMBER *25*
❖ 2 Corinthians 10, 11
❖ Psalms 127, 128

All our springs of thought and action are in the Holy Spirit: this is Christian freedom.

NOVEMBER *26*   ❖ 2 Corinthians 12, 13
                                 ❖ Psalms 129, 130

NOVEMBER *27*   ❖ Philippians 1, 2
                                 ❖ Proverbs 17

NOVEMBER *28*   ❖ Philippians 3, 4
                                 ❖ Proverbs 18

NOVEMBER *29*   ❖ Colossians 1, 2
                                 ❖ Proverbs 19

By word, deed and sign, Christians bear witness to the reality of the kingdom. How else will the world see the King?

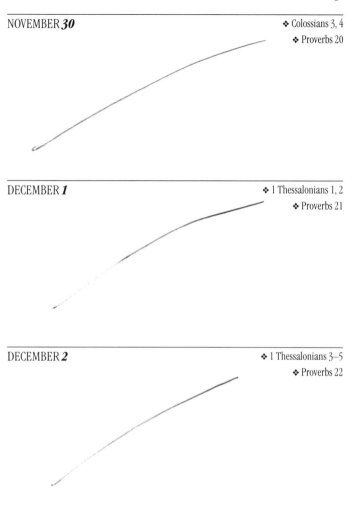

NOVEMBER **30**

❖ Colossians 3, 4
❖ Proverbs 20

DECEMBER **1**

❖ 1 Thessalonians 1, 2
❖ Proverbs 21

DECEMBER **2**

❖ 1 Thessalonians 3–5
❖ Proverbs 22

'"The world is charged with the grandeur of God." All things therefore are charged with love, are charged with God and if we know how to touch them, give off sparks and take fire, yield drops and flow, ring and tell of Him.'

Gerard Manley Hopkins

Christians live in the creative tension of being called out of the world and sent into the world.

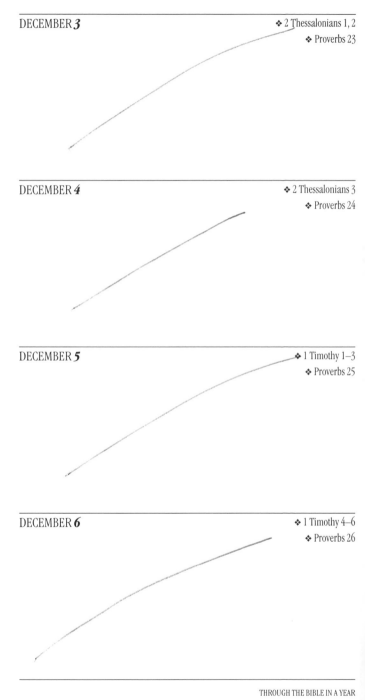

DECEMBER *3*	❖ 2 Thessalonians 1, 2
	❖ Proverbs 23

DECEMBER *4*	❖ 2 Thessalonians 3
	❖ Proverbs 24

DECEMBER *5*	❖ 1 Timothy 1–3
	❖ Proverbs 25

DECEMBER *6*	❖ 1 Timothy 4–6
	❖ Proverbs 26

The church is the Lord's experimental garden on earth, a fragment of the reign of God, something beautiful.

DECEMBER 7

❖ 2 Timothy 1, 2
❖ Proverbs 27

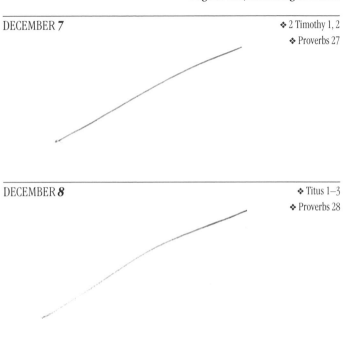

DECEMBER 8

❖ Titus 1–3
❖ Proverbs 28

The scriptures never allow us to float away on a spiritual cloud. Half the parables Jesus told are about the use of money. In fact, one out of every seven verses in the New Testament deals with money. Altogether, scripture offers about 500 verses on prayer and fewer than 500 on faith, while there are more than 2,000 verses on money! Martin Luther said, 'There are three conversions necessary: the conversion of the heart, the mind, and the purse!' Kingdom life is down-to-earth practical.

DECEMBER 9

❖ Philemon
❖ Proverbs 29

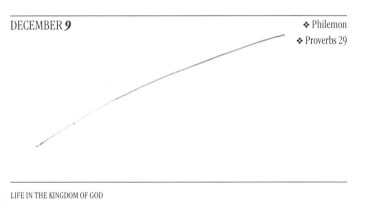

The ground of our faith is that God has given himself to us through Jesus Christ in the Holy Spirit.

DECEMBER **10**
❖ James 1, 2
❖ Proverbs 30

DECEMBER **11**
❖ James 3–5

DECEMBER **12**
❖ 1 Peter 1, 2
❖ Proverbs 31

DECEMBER **13**
❖ 1 Peter 3–5

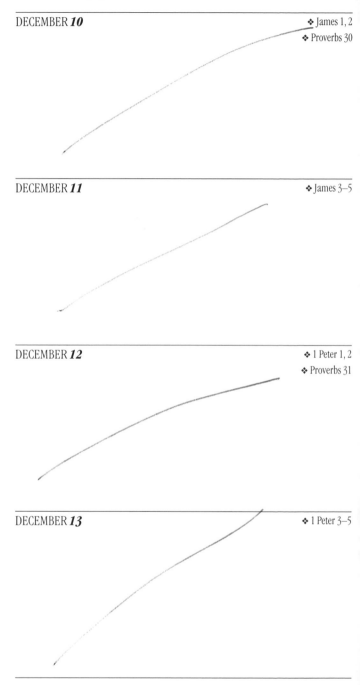

In Christ we have found the love that heals and sustains in all circumstances.

DECEMBER *14*

❖ 2 Peter 1
❖ Psalms 131, 132

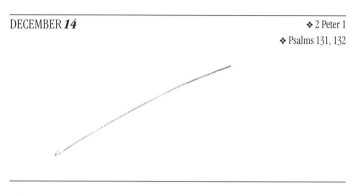

'Then I saw in my dreams that the Interpreter took Christian by the hand, and led him into a place where was a Fire burning against a wall, and one standing by it always casting much water upon it to quench it; yet did the fire burn higher and hotter. Then said Christian, "What means this?" ... so he had him about to the backside of the wall where he saw a man with a Vessel of Oil in his hand, of the which he did also continually cast (but secretly) into the fire.'

John Bunyan, *The Pilgrim's Progress*

DECEMBER *15*

❖ 2 Peter 2, 3
❖ Psalm 133

DECEMBER *16*

❖ 1 John 1, 2
❖ Psalms 134–136

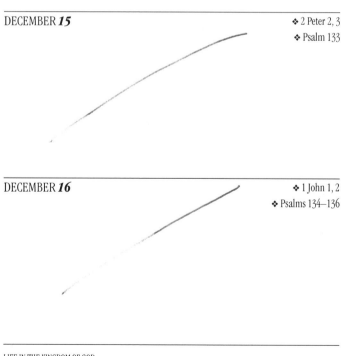

Sin is now unthinkable. Sin is what I do to God, violating his majesty, flouting his will.

DECEMBER *17* ❖ 1 John 3–5
❖ Psalms 137, 138

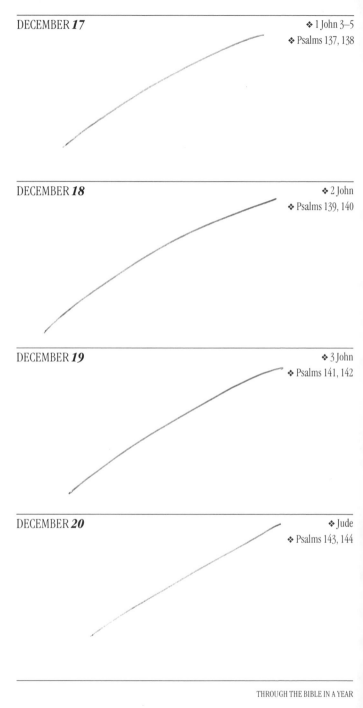

DECEMBER *18* ❖ 2 John
❖ Psalms 139, 140

DECEMBER *19* ❖ 3 John
❖ Psalms 141, 142

DECEMBER *20* ❖ Jude
❖ Psalms 143, 144

'...creation itself will be liberated from its bondage to decay and brought into the glorious freedom of the children of God' (Rom 8:21).

'At such moments, one suddenly sees everything with new eyes; one feels on the brink of some great revelation. It is as if we caught a glimpse of some incredibly beautiful world that lies silently about us all the time. I remember vividly my first experience of the kind when, as a boy, I came suddenly upon the quiet miracle of an ivy-clad wall glistening under a London street-lamp. I wanted to weep and I wanted to pray; to weep for the Paradise from which I had been exiled, and to pray that I might yet be made worthy of it.' **J W N Sullivan**

DECEMBER **21**

❖ Isaiah 56, 57
❖ Psalm 145
❖ Revelation 4

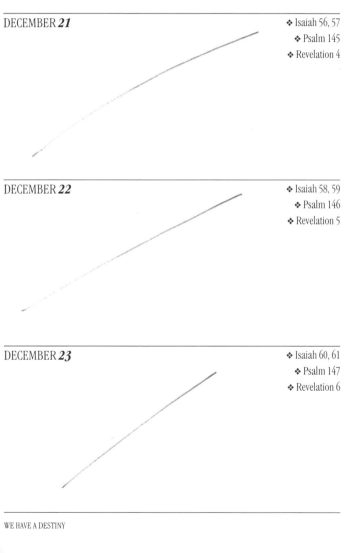

DECEMBER **22**

❖ Isaiah 58, 59
❖ Psalm 146
❖ Revelation 5

DECEMBER **23**

❖ Isaiah 60, 61
❖ Psalm 147
❖ Revelation 6

This world is still God's world, and the final victory lies with him and his covenant purposes for all creation.

DECEMBER *24*

❖ Isaiah 62, 63
❖ Psalm 148
❖ Revelation 7

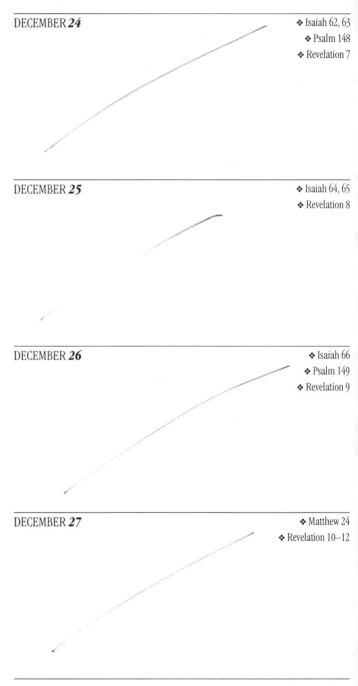

DECEMBER *25*

❖ Isaiah 64, 65
❖ Revelation 8

DECEMBER *26*

❖ Isaiah 66
❖ Psalm 149
❖ Revelation 9

DECEMBER *27*

❖ Matthew 24
❖ Revelation 10–12

'I saw the universe smiling.'

DECEMBER *28*

❖ Daniel 12
❖ Revelation 13, 14

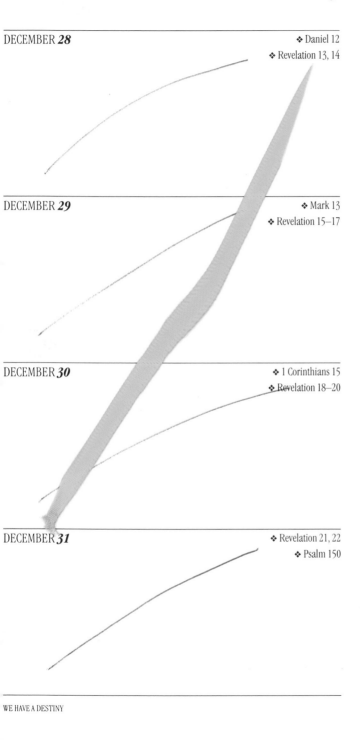

DECEMBER *29*

❖ Mark 13
❖ Revelation 15–17

DECEMBER *30*

❖ 1 Corinthians 15
❖ Revelation 18–20

DECEMBER *31*

❖ Revelation 21, 22
❖ Psalm 150

WE HAVE A DESTINY

If you've enjoyed this, try these...

Scripture Union produces four Bible reading guides to take you through the year, every year. Each has a distinctive identity, so that there is one to suit everybody.

Encounter with God offers in-depth study of God's word from respected Bible teachers. Review sections at the end of each week aid further reflection.

Daily Bread provides practical help in relating the Bible to your life every day. Information panels explain the world of the Bible.

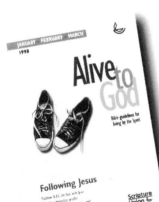

Alive to God uses creative reflections on the Bible to provide daily inspiration for prayer, praise, contemplation and action.

Closer to God will appeal to readers looking for a strong emphasis on the Holy Spirit and the power of God's word.

All notes are available quarterly, except Closer to God which is produced every two months. You can buy these notes from your local Christian bookshop, or from Scripture Union Mail Order, PO Box 764, Oxford, OX4 5FJ. Tel: 01865 716880